D1071328

How to Borrow Money From a Banker

Also by Roger Bel Air

Make a Fortune Buying Discounted Mortgages

How to Borrow Money From a Banker

A Business Owner's Guide

Roger Bel Air

American Management Association

This book is available at a special discount when ordered in bulk quantities. For information, contact Special Sales Department, AMACOM, a division of American Management Association, 135 West 50th Street, New York, NY 10020.

Library of Congress Cataloging-in-Publication Data

Bel Air, Roger.
How to borrow money from a banker.

Bibliography: p.
Includes index.
1. Commercial loans. I. Title.
HG1641.B45 1988 332.1'753 88-47705
ISBN 0-8144-5915-3

Printing number

10 9 8 7 6 5 4 3 2 1

To
Randy
and
Ronnie.
No one could ask for two finer brothers.

And to the thousands of entrepreneurs in this country who realize that the bankers making the lending decisions are not the same as the people writing the banks' advertisements.

Acknowledgments

First, I would like to thank Jerry Dootson and Bob Reimer, who, over a cup of coffee, suggested the idea of this book. Then, like true entrepreneurs, they asked me for a percentage of my book royalties for their ingenious suggestion.

Although an author spends many hours putting thoughts on paper, every book is the result of many people's efforts. Nick Briney, Dave Duryee, John Henderson, and Kathy Imdike had many suggestions, and each played an important role in this book. So did Art Mickel, Gerry Makus, and Ken Moultrie.

I especially want to thank Deborah Berger for her assistance in working on my manuscript; Dominick Abel, my literary agent; and Nancy Brandwein, my editor at AMACOM.

How to Borrow Money From a Banker is a reflection of my experience as a banker and, in recent years, as an entrepreneur dealing with lenders. I want to express appreciation to the many credit gurus with whom I have worked over the years. In particular, Terry Mix, Dick Rench, Richard Dunn, and Arland Hatfield were helpful in teaching me the ropes.

Finally I want to thank Seattle-First National Bank, my employer for over a decade. At one time, Seafirst was a fine organization.

Contents

INTRODUCTION:

What This Book Can Do for You

"The golden rule: Those who have the gold make the rules."

One expression you're probably familiar with is, "It takes money to make money." Both this and the epigram at the beginning of this introduction are probably truer today than ever before in the world of business. It's no surprise that, from time to time, three of every four businesses need to borrow money from a commercial bank. What may be a surprise is that few people ever feel comfortable dealing with a banker. The would-be borrower's effectiveness in the financial community is impaired because he doesn't understand the world of banking and the perspective of bankers.

Today I'm an independent businessman. Being in business for myself has many benefits, but one of the challenges I (and most other business owners) face from time to time is to borrow money. I don't necessarily find it easy to deal with bankers, but I have to admit I didn't always have this perspective. In fact, I really didn't learn about the challenges of working with lending officers until after I had left the world of banking.

After spending a number of years in the industry, I retired as a vice president with one of the largest banks in the country. In my last position as personal banking manager of the head office, I had responsibility for administering and supervising loans in excess of $50 million.

Over the years, I've learned that when you're in the process of borrowing money from a bank, it's not enough to talk the language of banking. You also need to know the unwritten rules, guidelines, and policies of the industry. How you handle yourself and the information you present to the banker affects whether you get your loan and the interest rate you're charged.

Because I understand the ins and outs of the banking system, it's easy for me to borrow money. I have the knowledge and background to get what I want. Bankers feel comfortable with me. But few other business owners or professionals have my background. I wrote this book to provide you the information you need to succeed with your banker—without spending years working as a loan officer.

This book is for any person who will ever need to borrow money from a bank. I show you the inside world of banking, teach you the unwritten rules of the industry, and prepare you for the questions a banker will ask. You'll learn everything you need to know *before* you approach a banker for a loan.

How to Borrow Money From a Banker is for anyone in business for himself or anyone who dreams of someday being an entrepreneur.

Names Have Been Changed to Protect the Innocent . . . and Guilty

The examples used in this book are based on my experiences as a banker and an entrepreneur. All names of individuals and companies have been changed. In addition, to preserve confidentiality in some cases, I have combined the elements of several individuals and situations to present a composite.

CHAPTER 1

The Predictable World of Banking

Tom Matheson is in a hurry. This husky plumbing contractor needs $30,000 to make his payroll and pay off his suppliers. He's working on a large apartment complex and can't afford to lose a single day of operation. What has caused the squeeze on his usually reliable cash flow? A major account is late paying his bill. He has assured Tom that the money will be in his hands next week, but Tom needs $30,000 today.

He jumps in his truck and runs down to his local bank, confident that his problem will be solved. After all, hasn't he had all his accounts—business and personal—at First National for the last ten years? And he never missed a payment on his truck loan.

Tom explains his problem to Rick Thornburg, one of the loan officers. Rick doesn't seem to understand that time is short. "Where are your financial statements?" he asks.

Tom is getting angry. "Financial statements! Who has time? I need to finish an apartment complex by next Wednesday!" He tells Rick to check his credit. But the banker, mindful of procedures and requirements, instead hands Tom a couple of blank forms. "Bring these back with your financial statements. Then we can talk," he says. "Call me when you're ready to make an appointment."

Tom storms out of the bank. Instead of a cashier's check, he has some blank forms in his hand and a sour feeling in his stomach. I'm not a deadbeat, he thinks, and I resent being treated this way. I don't have time for all this foolish paperwork. What am I going to do now?

Rick Thornburg doesn't feel so good either. He knows he has followed bank guidelines. The bank has to safeguard the depositors' money. Why did Tom Matheson wait until the last minute to come in for a loan? Did he really expect a cashier's check for $30,000 today? Tom doesn't seem to be a good planner or to understand how the bank works. Rick shakes his head and starts going through the mountain of paperwork on his desk.

Tom Matheson came up against a hard truth: Unless a banker is almost certain a loan will be repaid, the bank's money never leaves the vault. Since Tom had no understanding of how banks operate, he was unable to obtain the money he so desperately needed.

Three out of four business owners regularly borrow money from a bank. Clearly they need favorable banking relationships. Indeed, a good relationship is almost as important as having competent employees, competitive prices, and quality products or services.

To negotiate financing from a bank successfully, you need to know the unwritten rules of the industry. You need to understand the inner workings of the banking system and how the lending officer evaluates prospective borrowers. Once you understand these crucial elements, you are ready to obtain your loan. If you don't have this knowledge, you—like Tom Matheson—will become frustrated in your search for financial help.

How a Bank Makes a Profit

A bank makes a profit in a fairly straightforward manner. The public deposits money in a bank. Some of the money is deposited in checking accounts (sometimes called demand accounts, since they can be withdrawn on demand). Other funds are put in types of savings accounts that pay interest, such as passbook savings accounts or savings bonds, which pay a given rate of interest.

The bank then turns around and loans the depositors' funds to the public. In order for a bank to make a profit, the money on deposit is loaned at a higher rate of interest than what is paid to depositors.

Although a bank has income from the interest it earns on its loans, it also has the expense of paying interest on the money on deposit. The difference between the two covers the bank's overhead, and after that is met, the remainder is profit.

It's easy to see that bankers and borrowers need each other. When business owners borrow from a bank, both parties benefit: Owners get the money they need for their business ventures, and bankers earn interest on the funds borrowed. Although there are other sources of income for banks—revenues received from the service fees on checking accounts and the rental of safe deposit boxes are examples—but banks make most of their money by making loans.

Bankers vs. Borrowers

Stories about stodgy bankers are like belly buttons—everybody has one. On television and in movies, bankers are portrayed as stuffy creatures buttoned up in a dark blue or gray suit. And with a tight smile, they count, and then recount, every penny. The banker we see on the screen is not creative, personable, or warm. It's hard to imagine such an individual parachuting out of an airplane, enjoying a dirty joke, or sitting in a bathtub with a rubber duck.

Having been a banker, however, I can assure you that bankers are human beings. They have hobbies, drive automobiles, and watch TV. They even occasionally go to an R-rated movie just like the rest of us. Some bankers even have a great sense of humor. So why do so many people feel intimidated when dealing with bankers? For several reasons.

First, when most of us are trying to borrow money, we are coming from a position of need: We need to borrow money for a given purpose. Otherwise we wouldn't be at the loan officer's desk. As one customer said, "I only visit my dentist and my banker because of necessity. If I want a good time, I'll go play a round of golf with my buddies."

In addition to the fact that customers visit banks out of need, they are facing bankers who are in a position of control. A lending officer evaluates the financial health of the customer and assesses the overall situation. Then he decides whether the bank will participate in the project. Assuming the loan is made, everyone is happy. Should the loan request be declined, the applicant is disappointed and often feels that the banker has made an error in judgment.

Entrepreneurs and bankers look at a loan from different viewpoints. That's not to say that one is right and the other is wrong, just that the differences in perspective often cause a communication gap as wide as the Grand Canyon.

Take a look at the following lists to see just how different a typical entrepreneur and a banker can be from each other:

An entrepreneur is:	*A banker is:*
1. An opportunist: A risk taker who sees a need in the marketplace and sets out to fill it.	1. A caretaker of depositors' funds: Preservation of capital is the first concern.
2. An optimist.	2. A worrier: He focuses on "what can go wrong."
3. A doer: Someone who makes things happen.	3. An adviser, not a doer.
4. Someone who likes to be in control.	4. Someone who controls the purse strings.
5. A leader: Someone who directs a company.	5. Someone who is part of a large and often complex organization.
6. An independent decision maker: That's one of the reasons for going into business for oneself.	6. A team player: Someone who participates in decisions with others.
7. Often someone with a production or sales background.	7. Someone with a financial background.

8. Someone who looks at the big picture and concentrates on the forest, not each tree.
9. Someone with broad experience in one industry.
10. Someone who functions with limited regulations.
11. Someone with limited financing options (where else can he go?).

8. Someone who focuses on financial details: He analyzes the trees, not the forest.
9. Someone with specialized knowledge in finance.
10. Someone operating in a highly regulated industry.
11. Someone with many requests for depositors' money.

Let's compare these eleven characteristics:

1. *An opportunist vs. a caretaker of depositors' funds.* Entrepreneurs are looking for opportunities in the marketplace. They invest their own money and that of their creditors for personal gain. They thrive on the challenge of realizing their dreams. They are directly affected by the decisions they make.

Bankers are generally much more conservative. Unlike entrepreneurs, who are dealing with their own money, bankers are responsible for prudently investing depositors' funds. They spend a great deal of time reviewing applicants' requests and deciding whether the bank will participate in their projects. Their primary concern is to safeguard the bank's assets.

2. *An optimist vs. a worrier.* Entrepreneurs are optimists. They believe in themselves, their dreams, and their plans for the future. They believe that future profits will be available to repay the banks.

Bankers concentrate on the risks associated with the businesses and analyze what can possibly go wrong. I call this the "what-if" syndrome: "What if" this happens or "what if" that happens? Then how will the bank's depositors be repaid?

3. *A doer vs. an adviser.* I remember the businessman who said, "An entrepreneur's philosophy is 'Ready, fire, aim,' whereas a banker's thought process is 'Ready, aim, aim, aim.' "

It's tough to make it in the business world, especially if a company is small and trying to create a niche in the marketplace. Business owners need to be flexible. Sometimes decisions need to be made in a hurry.

Banking is a completely different type of industry. In addition to lending out depositors' money, bankers play the role of adviser and counselor. In a sense, good bankers are like external members of the management team. They provide fresh ideas and/or offer constructive criticism. Yet because they are outsiders, they are not involved in the process of carrying out managerial decisions.

4. *Someone who likes to be in control vs. one who needs to control the purse strings.* Business owners have confidence in their capabilities. They like to make decisions, and they want to be able to control their own destinies. Otherwise they wouldn't go into business for themselves. It's often difficult for them to approach a banker and ask for money. Part of the reason is the fear of rejection. It takes a strong person to start a business. For people with strong egos, relinquishing control is difficult. Since bankers hold the purse strings, they are in control of the situations.

5. *A leader vs. someone who is part of a bureaucracy.* Entrepreneurs have strong personalities. They are ambitious and have a clear vision of what they want to accomplish. They are men and women with missions and goals. As presidents or majority owners of their businesses, they have the responsibility of leading their companies. Their decisions directly affect their financial health and that of their employees.

By comparison, the banking industry is full of checks and balances. It processes a great deal of red tape. This is because banks are dealing with other people's money. Bankers are responsible for maintaining prudent behavior since they accept money from the public and then temporarily "rent out" these funds to others.

6. *An independent decision maker vs. a team player.* Successful entrepreneurs are able to make decisions that prove to be financially correct. They rely on their knowledge, background,

and instincts to help them in the competitive business environment. Decision making is usually centralized. As one managerial consultant said, "Many times an entrepreneur creates a one-rider horse." That is, the business is successful because of the abilities of its leader. Should something happen to the top decision maker, the future of the company is in jeopardy.

Banks are corporations owned by many stockholders. It would be nearly impossible for a bank president, or anyone else in the bank, to exercise the type of control that the owner of a privately held company can exercise. Rather than centralized decision making, committees make most of the major decisions. A banker is a team player who participates in decisions with others.

7. *Someone with a production or sales background vs. a person with a financial background.* Statistics show that most entrepreneurs come from either a production or a sales background. As such, they naturally have a bias toward their fields of expertise. For example, consider a baker who prides himself on making the best loaf of bread in town. If he decides to open up his own bakery, what will be his top priority? The answer is obvious: product quality. By contrast, a successful sales representative who opens a bakery is likely to emphasize sales. If profits are less than desired, she won't be as concerned with the quality of the product as with increasing the marketing efforts.

Only a small percentage of entrepreneurs have a financial background. Just as it's natural for someone to emphasize his field of expertise, at times it's also normal for an individual to underestimate or not fully understand the financial aspects of running a business.

A banker, on the other hand, primarily looks at the financial statements, his area of expertise. He has a narrow focus on the numbers. Trained in finance, a banker takes the position that all relevant activities of the company will show up in the figures.

8. *Someone who looks at the big picture vs. someone who focuses on the financial details.* Entrepreneurs understand the broad perspective of what needs to be done. The routine tasks and implementation details are often delegated to others.

Bankers have a greater analytical focus than most other people. Details are important to them. They are working in an industry where accuracy is a necessity. As one customer said, "I see the number $2,483 and think $2,500. A banker sees the same number and thinks $2,483.00." Perhaps he's right. Close attention to detail is part of being a banker.

Here's an example of these different perspectives: Linda Hale, owner of several grocery stores, decided to open another outlet. She needed $350,000 to meet part of the cost of opening the new store. The money was going to be used to buy inventory, shelving, light fixtures, and so on. Linda presented her banker with a breakdown of how the money would be spent. Part of the listing was a category of miscellaneous expenses for $50,000. From Linda's perspective, if she was good for the money, it didn't matter how she was going to spend the $50,000. Linda's banker had a different viewpoint. While the borrowing request made sense, it was important for him to know how the miscellaneous category was going to be spent.

9. *Someone with broad expertise in one industry vs. someone with specialized knowledge in finance.* Business owners look at the big picture. As one entrepreneur said, "I'm a jack of all trades and master of none." Well, he may be understating his abilities, but he is correct in declaring that a business owner wears many different hats. Entrepreneurs need to understand all aspects of their businesses. They need a broad knowledge and thorough understanding of marketing, production, personnel, and finance in order to orchestrate their companies' efforts.

By comparison, bankers have a specialized field of expertise: finance. A competent banker may know little about marketing or production because they aren't necessary to his job. Bankers are able to work with owners in many different industries because their basic financial knowledge applies to all businesses.

10. *An individual who functions with limited regulations vs. an individual operating in a highly regulated industry.* Most companies are able to operate with a minimum of government intervention. (Hospitals and utilities might be exceptions.) The management team sets policies and makes decisions depending on its desires and the needs of the marketplace.

By comparison, many laws and regulations govern the banking industry. Government agencies have many policies, rules, and guidelines that banks must follow. In addition, bank managements add more policies, making the organizations even more bureaucratic.

Some of these policies may make sense, and some may not. For instance, if you are creditworthy and buying a new car, a bank will be happy to finance it for you. It asks that you come up with a down payment and then use the car as collateral.

Now let's say that instead you pay for the car with money from your savings account. Then a couple of months later, you decide to replenish your savings account by getting a loan. You figure you will use the car as collateral. Your banker, however, says no.

Most banks don't make this kind of loan. Why? Bank policy. Banks solicit auto loans but don't make loans using cars as collateral when the money is going into a savings account for a rainy day.

Another example of what appears to be strange bank policy: Jeanne W. Brown, a wealthy restaurateur, was willing to deposit $1,200,000 in her bank savings account. She then wanted to borrow $1,000,000. The loan represented no risk to the bank because Jeanne was willing to pledge the savings account as collateral for the loan. Nevertheless, it took nine days after she presented her request before the banker could approve it because all loans of that size need to be approved by a loan committee. It didn't matter that the loan represented no risk to the bank since it was secured by the saving account. Again, bank policy dictated this bizarre behavior.

The bottom line: Tradition and policies are slow to change in the banking industry.

11. *Someone with limited financing options vs. someone with many requests for depositors' money.* If you are an entrepreneur, you probably need money. You need it to expand your business venture and to fulfill your dreams. It's likely that the piggy bank at home is empty and your mother and mother-in-law have said no for the eleventh time to your borrowing

request. In order for your company to grow and prosper, the ability to borrow money from a bank is almost a necessity.

On the other hand, the banking industry has many applicants for the funds they have to loan. They also have the responsibility of making sure that the depositors' money is given to creditworthy customers, those who will repay their loans on time.

After reviewing the typical differences between an entrepreneur and a banker, it's easy to understand how communication between two such individuals could be difficult. A business owner and a banker do not view the world from the same perspective.

While many people feel intimidated and frustrated when dealing with bankers, this doesn't have to be the case. You can avoid unpleasant experiences by choosing the right banker for your business and your needs.

Choosing the Banker Who's Right for You

When you choose a banker, you're choosing the products and services of the institution he represents, along with the personal abilities of the individual. Sometimes a business owner is dissatisfied with a particular banker or bank but resistant to the idea of changing financial institutions. In the past, bankers have promoted the idea that there is a benefit to maintaining a relationship with one bank over time. They've implied that loyal customers get better treatment—maybe even a lower interest rate.

Well, it would be nice if this reward for loyalty were true. But I consider it a myth. The length of time a customer has been with a bank has little to do with the quality of service received. What does matter is how much business a customer brings to the bank and how the person handles his financial affairs.

To choose a banker, start by getting recommendations and names of bankers from trusted business colleagues. Ask them why they're satisfied—and if there's anything they don't like about the service they're receiving. Then you can compare their comments with your financial needs. Should you want to meet a particular banker, perhaps your business associate would be willing to make an introduction. This is a great aid in beginning a positive relationship.

You deserve a banker who will provide high-quality service. Having spent years in the banking industry, I have a strong idea of what constitutes a competent banker. A good banker:

- Has a sincere interest in you and your business.
- Has a great deal of common sense and sees the big picture.
- Recognizes that financial reports are a valuable tool but realizes everything that happens inside a business is not reflected on the financial statements.
- Is a good communicator and doesn't use a lot of financial jargon.
- Visits your place of business to understand your financial needs better.
- Returns your telephone calls promptly.
- Provides direct and concrete answers (for example, he never says, "I don't know why the loan committee turned your request down.").
- Looks for creative financing options that meet your needs and still provide adequate protection for the bank (rather than simply turning down your loan request).
- Provides you insights into your company from what he learns by reviewing your financial statements.

Now that you know how a capable banker operates, you're ready to focus on the basics of borrowing money.

CHAPTER 2

The Basics of Borrowing

Borrowing money can be a blessing or a curse. Used wisely, a loan has several benefits, which I discuss in detail below. Too much borrowing, however, dilutes the stability of a company and can cause major financial problems.

I discuss when and how much you should borrow in Chapters 5 and 6; for now, let's look at the many advantages of borrowing money:

1. *Borrowed funds earn more than they cost.* Business people borrow money to increase profits. This is because the money invested in their businesses costs less than it earns. The main reason why most entrepreneurs borrow money is to increase their sales, which will then lead to higher profits.

2. *Credit is a matter of convenience.* It's much easier to pay for goods and services at scheduled intervals than to pay at the time the expense is accrued. A simple example is the long-distance telephone calls you make each month. Imagine if you had to pay each time you made a call. It's much easier to have a single bill to pay at the end of the month.

3. *Borrowing allows acquisition in the present rather than postponement of ownership.* Suppose home mortgages didn't exist and you had to accumulate the cash for the entire purchase price of a home before you could buy it. Probably you wouldn't be a home owner, and neither would I. Borrowing allows us to purchase a residence and then pay for it over many years.

The same is true for an entrepreneur who needs a new piece of equipment or some other item for the business. The bank's money allows him to purchase it now, when he really needs it, rather than waiting.

4. *Borrowing provides flexibility.* The cash needs of businesses go up and down over time. If a business owner supplies all of his own funds, cash may just sit idle. Since it's waiting to be used, it can't be invested for a long period of time. Therefore, the owner makes less profit than if the company could borrow money from a bank during times of peak monetary need.

Art Sather, a wheat farmer, plants his crop in the early spring and harvests it during the late summer. During this period, Art has many expenses and a sizable need for cash to pay for the planting, fertilizing, watering, and harvesting of the crop. After selling his wheat, Art has a large amount of cash. Usually it would be foolish for him to let most of this cash sit idly in a passbook savings account from late summer until it is needed the following spring.

5. *For many business owners, it's often easier to borrow than to put more money into their companies.* From time to time, most firms need additional cash. If the owners don't have additional money to put into their companies, they have a limited number of options. Maybe they can find acceptable partners who want to own part of their firms, but this is often difficult. Usually it's easier to borrow the money needed than it is to find a desirable partner looking to invest in a business.

These are the main advantages to borrowing. Most of us know when we need to borrow. Thus, the questions now become, How do we do it and what do bankers look for in approving loan requests?

My next point is very important: Many people think the borrowing of money is quantifiable. In other words, a banker sits down and puts certain facts and figures into a magical formula. Upon working through the formula, a decision is made of either thumbs up or thumbs down. *This is not true.*

The industry does have many guidelines and rules of thumb, but a banker's decisions are not bound by a formula. If a loan officer is convinced that the loan request will be repaid, then he'll give the money to the customer. If he is not certain that the business owner can or will repay the bank, the banker will decline the loan request and politely point the customer toward the door.

In making a decision, a lending officer starts with information supplied by the borrowers and then reviews information in files within the bank and data supplied by outside sources, such as reports from credit bureaus. Then the banker decides whether to approve or decline the applicant's request.

In a philosophical sense, all junior bankers are taught what to look for and how to judge prospective borrowers. In the banking community, this is referred to as the Six *C*'s of Credit.

The Six *C*'s of Credit

The Six *C*'s of credit are character, capacity, capital, collateral, conditions, and coverage. Let's take them one at a time.

Character

To bankers, *character* means the borrowers are people of their word. They are honest and reliable; they will do everything within their power to repay the debt. Of all the factors that come into the decision-making process, character is probably the most important. Bankers loan money only to people they believe intend to repay the bank.

Character lenders is a term used to describe some bankers. This type of banker relies heavily on instinct and the customer's reputation in the community. When presented with a loan application, a character lender sits back in his chair and asks: "Is ol' Joe good for the money?"

When I was a loan officer supervisor I liked to call this type of lending philosophy kiss-it-goodbye lending, because if the banker made a mistake, kiss-it-goodbye is exactly what you could do with the bank's money.

Years ago, character lenders were common in smaller communities. In this age of computers and large bureaucracies, however, most bankers rely on factors other than the applicant's character.

Capacity

Capacity is the word bankers use to describe the applicant's overall financial strength and track record. Being a successful entrepreneur is the result of many varied factors. Some talented people work hard and are richly rewarded for their efforts. Other people, despite their best efforts, have trouble keeping the doors open. It seems that they have a personal black cloud that follows them.

Bankers always look at an applicant's track record because they believe the future is probably going to be a reflection of the past. If in recent years an entrepreneur has been reasonably successful, it's likely that this trend will continue. In the coming months, the owner will probably have enough money to repay the bank. On the other hand, if the applicant has gone from one financial crisis to another, this trend is also likely to continue. Bankers believe that history repeats itself, and they always want to avoid problems.

Capital

Capital refers to the amount of equity a business owner has in the company. Bankers are much more comfortable loaning money to people who have a great deal of financial strength than to those deep in debt. The former have a much greater cushion of money beneath them should they run into rough financial waters.

Collateral

People who are viewed to be very creditworthy by banks do much of their borrowing using only their signatures. This type of loan is often called *unsecured* because no collateral (such as equipment, real estate, or accounts receivable) backs up or supports the borrower's signature.

Other borrowers are asked to pledge collateral or provide additional protection as a guarantee for the banks. Should they have difficulty repaying the loan, the collateral is sold. The cash received from the buyers goes to repay the loans.

Conditions

Conditions is the next *C*. Many decisions regarding the range and type of products to offer, the hiring of employees, and so on are within the control of a business owner; however, other factors that have an impact on the financial success of a company are outside the owner's control.

There could be a thousand different factors. Remember what happened when the price of oil went sky high in the 1970s? If you were in a business where the price of gas had an effect on your situation, the actions of the oil producers would have severely affected your financial picture. A banker needs to account for practically any condition that could sabotage your business.

Coverage

Finally we have *coverage*. When bankers refer to coverage, they are referring to insurance coverage. All of us are subject to perils such as damage due to a fire or a legal suit by an unhappy customer. Insurance protects us against these unforeseen events, which could dramatically cripple a business.

Insurance is not a luxury; it is a necessity. The amount of protection varies depending on the situation, but the coverage must be adequate.

The Bottom Line

The banker reviews the borrower's request as it relates to each of these six *C*'s of credit: character, capacity, capital, collateral, conditions, and coverage. The loan officer gains much of the information needed from the financial information provided by the borrower. It's important for business owners to understand the content of these financial reports and how a banker analyzes the facts and figures.

In the next few chapters, I'm going to explain—in plain English, not in banker's jargon—the financial information bankers need and how they use it.

CHAPTER 3

Measuring Your Financial Strength

A businessman once told me that he had three sets of financial statements: one for the IRS, which was pessimistic; one for the bank, which was optimistic; and the real set, which was more or less worthless. A lot of people share his opinion. Most men and women go into business with a limited knowledge of—and interest in—finance. Usually their background is in production or sales.

Over the years, I've worked with thousands of business owners. Some were on the verge of bankruptcy, and others were multimillionaires. *Almost without exception, every successful business owner understood his or her financial reports.*

This is not to say that to be successful you need an advanced degree in finance from Harvard. However, you do need to use a degree of common sense and have a basic understanding of the numbers.

I'm going to cover the fundamentals of financial reports for two reasons. First, you need to understand the information if you are going to communicate with bankers successfully. The world of banking is the world of finance. To negotiate financing, you need to play by the rules of the industry. A banker who has confidence in you, your abilities, and your company is likely to approve your financing request for a loan. If the banker doubts your abilities to repay the loan, then you are going to be turned down.

The second reason I'm discussing financial reports is to teach you a few basic principles that will help you become more successful. Financial reports are a valuable tool. They provide a look at what is happening inside a company.

Financial reports are a little like a résumé. Before hiring a new worker, an employer usually asks to see a résumé. The résumé doesn't tell the whole story, but it does provide a great deal of information about applicant's educational and work experience and thus enables the interviewer to form some preliminary opinions. The interviewer can relate the applicant's background and qualifications to the employment needs of the company.

Financial statements perform much the same function for bankers. When a prospective customer walks through the door, a banker knows little, if anything, about the individual or this person's firm. In fact, the lending officer may not even be familiar with the industry. But bankers are trained to read statements and interpret financial information. By reviewing the information and asking a few probing questions, a banker can learn a great deal and soon will have reasonably good insight into the company's track record and its financial success.

Financial reports can be used to assess how firms are doing, as well as to identify trends and concerns. They are beneficial to both bankers and owners. These reports are not difficult to understand. In fact, once you learn a few basic concepts, they are relatively easy to interpret.

There are two primary financial reports for any business: the balance sheet and the income statement. In this chapter, we are going to examine the balance sheet.

The Balance Sheet

I like to think of the balance sheet as being a financial snapshot of a business at a particular point in time. It lists what the business owns and outlines the amounts owed to others. The difference between the two is the owner's equity. This relationship can be expressed as follows:

Total funds invested in business	–	Funds supplied by creditors	=	Funds supplied by the owners

The world of finance has its own terminology. *Assets* describes what one owns. *Liabilities* describes what one owes to creditors. The remaining balance, or owner's equity, is called *net worth.* Therefore we have:

Assets – Liabilities = Net worth

Ralph Allen is the owner of ACME Manufacturing Co., a maker of women's suits. Ralph took over the ownership of ACME when his father retired. The company's most recent balance sheet is shown in Figure 3-1.

Assets and liabilities are listed in a particular order on the balance sheet, from most liquid to least liquid. Since cash is the most liquid asset, it is always the first category. Next is accounts receivable (money owed the firm), since it is soon to be converted into cash. Inventory is next; it is less liquid than cash or money owed. And so on down the line. *Current assets* are assets that will probably be converted into cash within the next year. Assets that don't fall into this current assets category are called *noncurrent* or *fixed assets.* (Equipment is an example of a fixed asset.)

Similar guidelines apply to liabilities. Current liabilities are those obligations that are expected to be paid during the coming year. If a liability is not a current liability, it is called a *long-term liability.* Mortgage payments, typically made over a number of years, fall in the category of long-term liabilities.

The numbers on a balance sheet provide only a limited amount of information. For instance, if a company has a net worth of $50,000, we don't know if that is good or bad. We can't tell a lot by just looking at a single number. But once we start making comparisons to other figures, the number starts having some meaning. One of the best ways to understand the meaning of any figure is to make comparisons with past years.

Figure 3-1. ACME Manufacturing Co. balance sheet.

ACME MANUFACTURING CO.
Balance Sheet
December 31, 19X5*
($ in 000s)

ASSETS	
Cash	$ 85
Accounts receivable	355
Inventory	585
Prepaid expenses	75
Total current assets	1,100
Net fixed assets	210
Other assets	100
TOTAL ASSETS	$1,410
LIABILITIES	
Accounts payable	$ 293
Other current liabilities	441
Total current liabilities	734
Long-term liabilities	86
TOTAL LIABILITIES	$ 820
Net worth	$ 590
TOTAL NET WORTH AND LIABILITIES	$1,410

* 19X5 means it could represent any decade.

How Comparisons Show Trends

If a company's net worth last year was $100,000 and this year the net worth is merely $50,000, the natural question is,

Why the dramatic drop? Did the firm lose a considerable amount of money? Or is there some other reason, such as that the owner took some money out of the company?

On the other hand, let's suppose that the net worth of the firm was only $25,000 last year, and the year before it was only $10,000. Should that be the case, it appears that the company is making progress.

You can see the need to examine financial information by looking at trends. (This is possible only if the firm has been in business for several years.) Once you see the trend, you can focus on the causes or the reasons behind the changes. This process provides insight into the true condition of a company.

To make it a little easier to see the trends, bankers often transfer the balance sheet figures from several years to a single piece of paper. The term used for this combined group of numbers is a *spreadsheet.* Looking at a spreadsheet makes it much easier to observe trends. Some astute business people put key financial figures on a graph so they can see the changes.

Relationships on the Balance Sheet

While viewing trends is important, perhaps even more valuable is the interrelationships of the categories on the balance sheet. For instance, two firms might have the same net worth, but the financial condition of their companies may be completely different. Their assets and liabilities could be as follows:

	Assets	–	*Liabilities*	=	*Net worth*
Adams Co.	$125,000	–	$ 25,000	=	$100,000
Jones & Son	$900,000	–	$800,000	=	$100,000

There is a considerable difference in the financial composite of the two companies. Adams Co. is relatively debt free. It owes only $25,000. Jones & Son, on the other hand, is heavily in debt.

A banker examining these two companies would look at the amount of net worth in each company compared to what it owes others. Bankers frequently express the relationship between two numbers in the form of a ratio. With these two companies above, we would have for Adams Co., $25,000/$100,000 = .25, and for Jones & Son, $800,000/$100,000 = 8.

Comparing the ratio of .25 to 8 makes it easier to understand the financial position of these two companies. It is much simpler than trying to comprehend the relationship of the different numbers.

The number of possible financial ratios is practically endless. Most bankers and financial managers, however, find it's necessary to use only a few ratios.

When looking at the trends and ratios, bankers might want to compare a company's figures with those of other firms in the same industry. In other words, is a ratio of 2.0 good? Or should it be 3.0 or something else? The norms or averages in an industry affect a banker's perception of your business.

Many times bankers know if the ratio is or isn't reasonably close to industry standards. If they don't know or aren't sure, they probably will refer to a reference manual such as *Annual Statement Studies* published by Robert Morris and Associates. Many industry ratios are also available at public libraries and from many trade associations. (Appendix C lists various common sources of this information.)

Reviewing the Balance Sheet

When bankers look at a balance sheet, their focus is on two things: the company's solvency and its safety. These two words can be defined as follows:

- *Solvency:* The company's ability to pay its bills.
- *Safety:* The firm's ability to withstand adversity.

To help you understand how bankers review a balance sheet, I'm going to use some examples. A banker's analysis is the same regardless of the size of the company. It doesn't matter if the company's net worth is $2,200, $220,000, or $2,200,000. So if the examples I use in this book are larger or smaller than what you are familiar with, simply add or drop a couple of zeros.

Solvency: The Ability to Pay the Bills

Let's start with solvency, a term dear to a banker's heart. When measuring a company's ability to pay back its obligations, the key is to look at the available financial resources. An important relationship exists between current assets and current liabilities.

This relationship is called the *current ratio* and can be stated as follows:

$$\text{Current ratio} = \frac{\text{Current assets}}{\text{Current liabilities}}$$

In lay language, the current ratio, sometimes called the *working capital ratio,* simply means a certain amount of money is available to cover each and every dollar of bills due.

The spreadsheet for Ralph Allen's ACME Manufacturing, Co. (Figure 3–2) shows the company's annual balance sheets over the last few years. Dividing the current assets by the current liabilities gives the current ratio for ACME. In recent years it has been as follows:

	19X2	*19X3*	*19X4*	*19X5*
Current assets =	$906	$964	$1,010	$1,100
Current liabilities	$648	$688	$674	$734
Current ratio =	1.40	1.40	1.50	1.50

The amount of resources available to pay bills coming due in coming months has increased over the past four years. In 19X5 there was $1.50 of current assets to pay every dollar of current liabilities. This figure compares with $1.40 in 19X2. Thus the trend is relatively stable and slightly improving. However, what's considered a good or acceptable ratio depends to a large degree on the particular industry. A current ratio of 2.5 might be about average in one industry, and 1.3 would be closer to the mark in another industry.

Figure 3-2. ACME Manufacturing Co. income statement balance sheet spreadsheet.

ACME MANUFACTURING CO.
Income Statement Balance Sheet Spreadsheet
($ in 000s)

	19X2	19X3	19X4	19X5
ASSETS				
Cash	$ 72	$ 74	$ 70	$ 85
Accounts receivable	381	339	334	355
Inventory	389	483	536	585
Prepaid expenses	64	68	70	75
Total current assets	906	964	1,010	1,100
Net fixed assets	190	190	195	210
Other assets	66	81	88	100
TOTAL ASSETS	$1,162	$1,235	$1,296	$1,410
LIABILITIES				
Accounts payable	$ 260	$ 275	$ 270	$ 293
Other current liabilities	388	413	404	441
Total current liabilities	648	688	674	734
Long-term liabilities	67	53	82	86
TOTAL LIABILITIES	$ 715	$ 741	$ 756	$ 820
Net worth	$ 447	$ 494	$ 540	$ 590
TOTAL NET WORTH AND LIABILITIES	$1,162	$1,235	$1,296	$1,410

A banker probably would want to know how this 1.50 figure compares to other firms in the clothing industry. Are

ACME's numbers near the norm, or are they considerably different? Looking in Robert Morris & Associates' *Annual Statement Studies,* the banker would learn that the industry average for companies the same size as ACME is 1.45. This information is helpful; it shows that ACME is slightly more solvent than the average company in the industry. It has $1.50 of current assets to pay each dollar of current liabilities—5 cents above the norm for the industry.

All bankers consider the current ratio important and will examine it. Some bankers also use a slightly tougher test known as the *quick ratio* to evaluate the solvency of a company.

The quick ratio differs from the current ratio in a fundamental way: Instead of looking at all current assets to pay short-term obligations, one can consider only cash and accounts receivable when figuring the quick ratio. This ratio is a more stringent test than the current ratio and is a good indicator of the firm's liquidity. Therefore, we now have:

$$\text{Quick ratio} = \frac{\text{Cash} + \text{Accounts receivables}}{\text{Current liabilities}}$$

Using our spreadsheet, we have the following:

		19X2	*19X3*	*19X4*	*19X5*	*Industry Norm*
Cash + Accounts receivable	=	$453	$413	$404	$440	
Current liabilities		$648	$688	$674	$734	
Quick ratio	=	.70	.60	.60	.60	.70

In 19X5 we see that ACME has .60 cent of cash and accounts receivables to pay the current liabilities. In the highly unlikely event that all creditors demanded—and received—immediate payment, the firm could be forced to go out of business. This is true even though ACME is profitable and has a solid net worth.

ACME's quick ratio of .60 is below the industry norm of .70; however, there is not enough of a difference to be significant, so in all likelihood ACME's banker won't become too concerned.

ACME's 19X5 current assets consist of four different assets:

Cash	$ 85
Accounts receivable	355
Inventory	585
Prepaid expenses	75
Total current assets	$1,100

The current ratio tells us that the company has plenty of current assets. The quick ratio, however, indicates that the company might be a little short on cash and accounts receivable. Considering these facts, a banker might wonder if ACME is a little heavy in inventory and/or prepaid expenses. Bankers may ask Ralph some questions about his inventory. Is the inventory level higher than normal? How is it valued? With changing clothing styles, will any of it have to be sold to wholesalers at reduced prices? Depending on the answers given, the banker may be satisfied or may probe for more information.

So far we really don't have enough information about ACME's financial situation to draw any definite conclusions. We do know, however, that the company is in a good position to pay its bills.

Safety: How Safe Is Safe?

In addition to solvency, the other key relationship all bankers focus on the balance sheet is the *safety* of the company. In bankers' terms, safety refers to the company's ability to withstand financial adversity. The best way to measure safety is simply to look at the relationship between money owed to creditors and the owner's equity. This comparison is called the *debt-to-worth ratio:*

$$\text{Debt-to-worth ratio} = \frac{\text{Total debt}}{\text{Net worth}}$$

The higher the ratio is, the more money the owner owes

in relation to the funds invested in the business. A high ratio means more risk for the business owner and creditors.

Using our spreadsheet for ACME, we have the following:

		19X2	*19X3*	*19X4*	*19X5*	*Industry Norm*
Total debt / Net worth	=	$715 / $447	$741 / $494	$756 / $540	$820 / $590	
Debt-to-worth ratio	=	1.60	1.50	1.40	1.39	1.80

The relationship of money supplied by the creditors to the resources of ACME has declined over the past four years. The debt-to-worth relationship is well below the norm for the industry. This means that ACME uses its creditors' money much less than the typical company in the industry does. In fact, Ralph owes about $1.39 for every dollar of capital invested compared to about $1.80 owed by the competition.

If this ratio were 3.0 or 4.0, the banker might have a concern with Ralph's use of "other people's money." However, ACME is well within accepted guidelines, and the banker will consider it a "safe" firm.

By now you've probably figured out that, as business people, we all strive for an "optimal financial balance." This is much better than running a company where the ratio represents extremes. For instance, an extremely low debt-to-worth ratio might mean that the creditor's position is very safe. The owner, however, wants to maximize profits while accepting a reasonable amount of risk. As such, it makes sense for an owner to use a certain amount of "other people's money" to increase the potential for profits.

While it varies from industry to industry, the average debt-to-worth ratio for most firms runs about 2 or 3 to 1. This means that a company owes creditors about $2 or $3 for every dollar the owner has invested in the firm.

To sum up the balance sheet: Bankers wants to know two factors when they look at this financial report. First, they want to know the solvency (the ability to pay its bills) of the company. Second, they want to know if the creditor's money is safe (if the business can withstand a rough financial storm without failing).

With ACME we have seen that it has more than enough money to pay its bills. We also know that Ralph, the owner, has maintained a conservative posture toward the use of "other people's money."

We're now ready to focus on the other key financial report, the income statement.

CHAPTER 4

Looking at Your Profit Picture

The income statement, the second essential financial report, shows the profitability of a company over time. Sometimes called a *profit and loss statement,* the income statement can cover any time frame; typically it reports the firm's activity for one year. The year-end income statement for ACME Manufacturing Co. is shown in Figure 4–1.

All income statements start with the revenues or sales produced by a firm and end with the after-tax profit. The names of the other categories may vary somewhat depending on the particular industry.

Expenses are usually divided into two major categories. *Cost of goods sold* is often used to describe expenses that directly relate to the product(s) or services provided. For a manufacturing company, such expenses would include materials, labor, and freight used in the production of the products. Subtracting the cost of goods sold from the company's sales results in what bankers call the *gross profit.*

The second expense category, frequently called *general and administrative expenses,* refers to charges that come with the normal operation of running a business. Utilities, office supplies, and advertising are examples.

By subtracting the cost of goods sold and general and administrative expenses from a company's sales, you are left with the *operating profit.*

Figure 4-1. ACME Manufacturing Co. income statement.

ACME MANUFACTURING CO.
Income Statement
December 31, 19X5
($ in 000s)

Net sales	$3,294
Cost of goods sold	2,458
Gross profit	836
<u>EXPENSES</u>	
General and administrative expenses	780
Total operating expenses	780
Operating profit	56
Other income	15
Net profit before tax	71
Income tax	21
Net profit	$ 50

Sometimes there is a third expense category on the income statement: *other income and expenses.* This category applies to any extraordinary gain or expense. For example, if a company sells a building, the substantial gain realized from this sale comes under "other income and expenses." In another case, a company might settle a lawsuit, perhaps incurring a major expense. These types of activities are unique. That is why they are reported in a separate expense category.

As with the balance sheet, most bankers consolidate the individual income statements on a spreadsheet. That way they can see the trends. It's also common for bankers to measure a company's financial results against industry standards. Once again, the easiest way to do this is with ratios.

Most bankers use two key ratios to measure the profitability of a firm: the gross profit margin and the net profit margin.

Gross Profit Margin: Measuring Production Efficiency

The gross profit is what remains after subtracting the cost of goods sold from the company's sales. The *gross profit margin* is the relationship between the gross profit and sales. It can be stated:

$$\text{Gross profit margin} = \frac{\text{Gross profit}}{\text{Sales}}$$

Perhaps the easiest way to understand the gross profit margin is to think of it this way: For every dollar of sales, how many cents remains after production? This is the same as the gross profit margin. As with all other financial ratios, the overall trend and comparison with industry standards is the banker's primary focus.

The income statements for ACME Manufacturing are shown in Figure 4–2. In determining the gross profit margin we have the following:

		19X2	*19X3*	*19X4*	*19X5*	
Gross profit	=	$416	$449	$683	$836	
Sales		$1,542	$1,708	$2,625	$3,294	
Gross profit margin	=	27.0	26.3	26.0	25.4	28.4

There is a trend for ACME, and it isn't good: The gross profit margin ratio has steadily declined in each of the past four years. This means that for each dollar of sales generated, less and less is available to cover overhead and profits. We also could say that the cost of production for each dollar of sales has gone up each year. Both statements mean exactly the same.

It is equally significant that comparison with the industry norm shows competitors are doing a much better job than ACME at keeping down production costs of their clothing. ACME has only 25.4 cents out of every sales dollar to cover overhead and contribute to profits. The competition averages 28.4 cents. Three cents doesn't sound like a lot. But when you work out the actual figures, you'll see that it is. In fact, since sales are over $3 million, it amounts to over $90,000 (.03 times sales of $3 million).

What could be causing the drain on ACME's profits? Several factors are possible culprits. Maybe ACME's pricing is too low. Perhaps the company is paying too much for its raw materials. Its marketing efforts may be stalled. An outdated plant with inefficient operations could be to blame. There could be a single element affecting ACME . . . or several contributing causes that add up to financial trouble.

A smart banker would ask Ralph, the owner, some probing questions: Has he identified the problem? Is he taking corrective action? Or is he unaware that the company is not running as effectively as it should? The loan officer would want to know if Ralph is on top of the situation.

Figure 4-2. ACME Manufacturing Co. income statement balance sheetspread sheet.

ACME MANUFACTURING CO.
Income Statement Balance Sheet Spreadsheet
($ in 000s)

	19X2	19X3	19X4	19X5
Net sales	$1,542	$1,708	$2,625	$3,294
Cost of goods sold	1,126	1,259	1,942	2,458
Gross profit	416	449	683	836
EXPENSES				
General and administrative expenses	379	408	641	780
Total operating expenses	379	408	641	780
Operating profit	37	41	42	56
Other income	13	12	12	15
Net profit before tax	50	53	54	71
Income tax	7	6	8	21
Net profit	$ 43	$ 47	$ 46	$ 60

Net Profit: A Look at the Bottom Line

The *net profit margin* shows what remains after paying all expenses except income taxes. You may wonder why this ratio is figured before taxes since it may seem to make more sense to calculate the ratio after taxes have been paid. Well, taxes can vary from firm to firm for a variety of reasons, so using the pretax profit figure is common.

This ratio, sometimes called the *return on sales,* can be stated:

$$\text{Net profit margin} = \frac{\text{Net profit before tax}}{\text{Sales}}$$

For ACME Manufacturing we have:

		19X2	*19X3*	*19X4*	*19X5*	*Industry Norm*
Net profit before tax / Sales	=	$50 / $1,542	$53 / $1,708	$54 / $2,625	$71 / $3,294	
Net profit margin ratio	=	3.2	3.1	2.1	2.2	2.7

In 19X5, for every dollar of sales, ACME had about 2.2 cents left over before paying taxes. Unfortunately, over the years, ACME's net profit margin has declined. In 19X2 and 19X3, Acme's net profit margin was well above the industry's average. During the past three years, however, the net profit margin has dropped from 3.2 to 2.2. This represents one full penny for every dollar of sales. ACME's production expenses have been higher than the industry average, so it's not surprising profits are low.

On the surface a net profit margin of .5 cent per dollar of sales (the difference between ACME's 2.2 and the industry norm of 2.7) doesn't sound like much. Yet when you consider the sales level of ACME, the company should be earning an additional $16,500 annually (figured by multiplying the sales of $3.3 million times .5 cent).

By comparing the gross profit margin ratio and the net profit margin ratio, we can tell that Ralph is doing a good job of controlling overhead and administrative expenses. For every dollar of sales, the gross profit margin is below the competition by 3 cents. Yet the net profit ratio only misses the mark by one-half cent.

Depending on the banker, the amount of money Ralph wants to borrow, and related factors, the banker may or may not spend more time reviewing the company's income statement. The banker might spend more time looking at individual expenses and studying the report to learn more about the company's profit situation. However, all bankers use the gross and net profit margin ratios to look at a company's profit situation.

Return on Assets: How Well Is a Company Using Its Resources?

Two additional ratios are useful in measuring how effectively and efficiently a company is operating.

The first is the *return on assets ratio,* sometimes called ROA. Assets are the resources of any company. They are what management uses to generate sales. After expenses are paid, whatever remains is profit. We can see that profits are actually a reflection of how well a company is using its assets. So the logical question that follows is: Are the company's assets being used effectively, or is there excessive waste?

The return on assets ratio can give us insight into this question. It is stated:

$$\text{Return on assets} = \frac{\text{Net profit before tax}}{\text{Total assets}}$$

When we look at ACME, we have the following from the spreadsheet:

		19X2	*19X3*	*19X4*	*19X5*	*Industry Norm*
Net profit before tax / Total Assets	=	\$50 / \$1,162	\$53 / \$1,235	\$54 / \$1,296	\$71 / \$1,410	
Return on assets	=	4.3	4.3	4.2	5.0	5.5

ACME's return on assets is well below the industry norm. With what we know about this company, this figure shouldn't come as too much of a surprise. The net profit per dollar of the company assets has declined over the past four years. For every dollar of assets, the company is getting profits below the industry average of 5.5 cents. This tells us that the company's resources (assets) are not being used efficiently to generate sales and profits.

Finally, I always look at the *return on investment ratio,* sometimes referred to as ROI.

Return on Investment: Is the Owner's Equity Earning an Adequate Return?

In addition to being compensated for their time and effort, business owners should receive a reasonable return on their investment. What I'm talking about is an owner's capital in his company. For instance, an owner who is earning only 2 or 3 percent on equity might want to consider investing equity elsewhere. (The same money even in a passbook savings account would be earning more than this.)

It's smart for the owner to compare return on equity to other investment opportunities in the marketplace. This way the owner knows if the business venture is a sound investment.

The return on investment ratio tells us the kind of return a business owner is obtaining on equity. The ROI is as follows:

$$\text{Return on investment} = \frac{\text{Net profit before tax}}{\text{Net worth}}$$

For ACME we have:

		19X2	*19X3*	*19X4*	*19X5*	*Industry Norm*
Net profit before tax / Net worth	=	$50 / $447	$53 / $494	$54 / $540	$71 / $590	
Return on investment	=	11.2	10.7	10.0	12.0	14.7

The ROI for ACME Manufacturing is well below the industry norm. This information substantiates what we already know. Most owners in the industry are earning almost 15 percent on their capital. Ralph is struggling to earn 12 percent.

What We've Learned About ACME

We have just learned a great deal about ACME Manufacturing and its owner, Ralph Allen. By starting with the balance sheet, we learned that the company has plenty of financial resources to pay its bills. However, the quick ratio, while acceptable, raises a possible red flag relating to the company's inventory.

As we looked at the safety of the company, we learned that Ralph has a conservative attitude in this area. The company does not have many debts relative to the amount of capital invested by the owner. This is especially true compared with other firms in the industry.

Then we moved on to the revenue and expense side of the company and gained some valuable insights into the company's financial situation. Although the company might be financially solid and made $50,000 last year, it is operating well below the industry's average.

In our analysis, we see that Ralph could improve his profit picture dramatically by working on those items that include the cost of goods sold. If the gross profit margin ratio were increased to the industry's norm, profits for ACME would improve substantially.

The costs associated with the overhead and administrative side of the business appear to be kept well under control.

Finally, we looked at how effectively the company is using its resources (assets) and the return the owner is receiving on his equity. Our findings in these areas were consistent with what we expected.

In a nutshell, we see that the company is solvent and safe and that the owner is conservative. Yet because of the concerns about the cost of goods sold, Ralph is not earning as much money as he should.

So there you have it. By looking at the trends, applying a few ratios, and using common sense, we have learned a great deal about ACME Manufacturing—without stepping inside the plant.

Financial Reports Are Not Enough

Many bankers, however, spend too much effort analyzing financial statements at the expense of other considerations—like getting to know their customer's needs.

Whenever I talk to a group of bankers, I always encourage them to get out from behind the desk and visit their customer's place of business. It helps give them a "real-world" perspective rather than relying so heavily on the numbers before them.

Good bankers do exactly what I'm suggesting. They realize that financial reports are an important tool. Yet they also know that being a capable banker is more than being able to analyze a financial report. They get to know their customers as people. They blend the elements of common sense, people skills, and what they learn from digesting financial data.

CHAPTER 5

Planning Your Financial Needs

Some people think that there is a general rule of thumb about how much they can borrow from the bank. For instance, they think that a banker will loan them perhaps 40 percent of their net worth or that they can borrow an amount equal to their current assets. This is not true. The banking industry doesn't work that way.

The process starts with applicants' financial needs. Bankers review those needs and then decide if they want to participate in the business venture. Borrowers therefore do not have a certain "borrowing capacity." Instead, bankers base their decisions about whether to grant or decline loan requests by looking at the applicant's financial strength and the circumstances surrounding the situation. For instance, a banker may be willing to lend a customer only $30,000 on the basis of her signature. On the other hand, should the customer's rich aunt be willing to pledge her savings account as collateral, the banker may be willing to lend the same person $1,000,000.

Sometimes business owners don't know their financial needs; they know only that they have bills to pay and no money in their checking account. Borrowing enough money to pay their bills might solve the problem—but next month they might face the same situation.

In order for borrowers to ask for the right amount of money, they have to understand their financial needs. Receiving too little money causes owners to operate on a shoestring. On the other hand, borrowing too much is wasteful; it causes higher interest expenses and reduces profits.

Before business owners can understand and recognize their needs, they must perform an essential task: planning.

Planning: Today and Tomorrow

Planning isn't necessarily fun or easy. In fact, at times it can be difficult because you are dealing with the uncertainty of the future. Nevertheless, planning is vital. Spending a few minutes planning can save you a great deal of time and effort in the future. It gives direction to any company. It's also a great tool to use in making day-to-day decisions.

Planning helps determine your financial needs. One business tycoon told me, "The planning I do for my company is like a road map in my car. After deciding my destination, it's a great aid in helping me get there."

Planning consists of looking at both short- and long-term goals. Some experts suggest having broad five-year objectives and more tangible, clearly defined goals earmarked for the next two years. Most important are the specific objectives you intend to reach during the coming year. Here are some factors to consider when starting the planning process:

1. *What are your personal goals and desires?* While all of us want to grow and prosper as individuals, we have only so much time and so much energy. So we must choose priorities.

Ken Quarles and Rick Fortner each owns a pizza parlor. Although both operate the same type of business, their goals in life are completely different. Ken wants to be a millionaire and retire by the time he is 40. He works hard and puts in long hours at his shop in pursuit of his ambitious goal. Rick is more interested in just making a comfortable living. Money isn't that important to him. He prefers to spend time with his family. Rick's real joy in life is coaching his son's soccer team.

2. *What is the business environment?* What are the trends in the industry? Is competition expected to increase or be about

the same in the near future? What about the economic conditions? Are they bright, or are there clouds on the horizon? Being able to weather changes in your customers' buying desires and habits is essential for long-term success.

Carol Albo learned that lesson well. Her company has distributed fine china and crystal for the last three decades. In recent years, many people have been willing to spend more to enjoy the high-quality, expensive products she distributes. Her business is booming, and the outlook for the next couple of years appears to be very promising.

Yet in the 1960s Carol's future was anything but bright. Then, many people focused their energies on social concerns and being close to nature. Inexpensive pottery was more popular than fancy china and crystal. Yet styles and tastes change over time, and she is now very successful.

3. *What are the strengths and weaknesses of your business?* What particular strengths can you capitalize on to improve your position in the marketplace? What are your company's shortcomings? How would you access your facilities, the quality of management, the ability to replace a key employee, and the products or services offered to your customers?

Being able to analyze your business honestly and critically is of great value, as Dexter Talcott knows. For the past 19 years, Dexter has owned and operated a real estate office in a small town of about 20,000 people. In evaluating his company, Dexter is convinced that its primary strength is the firm's favorable reputation in the community. His company is known for providing good-quality service. Dexter has bolstered this image by serving as a member of the city council and participating in various service organizations. As the owner of the company, he thinks it is important for him to maintain a high profile.

Like every other company, Dexter's firm also has its weaknesses. Within the last year, the number of sales agents has dropped from 10 to 6. If he wants to maintain the sales activity of recent years, he will have to hire and train additional sales staff. This will take a considerable amount of his time in coming months and cut into his community activities.

Since Dexter feels his firm's success is heavily dependent on community involvement, he may need to make some managerial decisions. Some of his options could include hiring a manager to assist with the training, encouraging staff members to become more involved in the community, or sponsoring some type of local activity to promote the name of his firm.

4. *What are the goals and objectives of your company?* Typically owners pick certain levels of profit and/or sales as goals. Many entrepreneurs also like to target specific goals and objectives for each department within their organizations. It helps build a team effort and encourages everyone to work together toward reaching common objectives.

Research has shown that goals should be measurable and specific. Thus, reaching a goal is not a matter of relying on subjective judgment.

Making goals specific is something Dave Normile does well. Dave has several well-defined targets for the coming year: He wants profits for his company, Normile's Painting, Inc., to increase to $75,000 and sales to hit $1,100,000. His commercial waterproofing and painting firm has been in business for five years, and Dave is all too aware that a new warehouse is long overdue. He plans to start construction on the new building in the coming year. Also, Dave knows that he needs to spend more time soliciting new accounts. In the next couple of months, he plans to train a new foreman. This will permit him to spend less time out in the field and more time developing new business.

After you've gone through the analysis outlined by these questions, you'll be ready to prepare some projections.

Figures for the Future

Some bankers frequently request projections; others do not. As a rule, the more money requested or the longer the period required to repay the bank, the more likely is the need for projections. I wouldn't even consider requesting a sizable amount of money (i.e., $50,000 or more) without providing financial projections for the banker.

There are basically three different types of projections: the cash budget, the projected income statement, and the projected balance sheet. In financial circles, you often hear the terms *pro forma* and *projected.* Both mean the same. All three projections are relatively easy to prepare, but they do require some time and effort.

Of the three projections, the cash budget is the most important for seasonal needs because it represents the flow of funds through the company.

Here's an example. Let's say you're a self-employed football program salesman. The morning of the big game, you give cash to the distributor for a supply of programs. A few hours later, you sell the programs to the football fans for cash, and then your work for the day is complete. In this case, when sales and expenses occur, so does a corresponding change in your cash position. Unlike this example, however, most businesses neither immediately spend cash when they have an expense nor receive cash as soon as they make a sale.

A more common situation involves a wholesaler. When a customer places an order, a sale is registered, and the customer is billed for payment. At the time of the sale, the firm doesn't yet have the cash from the customer; instead it simply has a promise to pay. Also, each day, expenses (such as the cost of goods bought from the manufacturer) are incurred. So in this case, the firm's cash position is much different from what it is when the sales and expenses occur.

Another example illustrates how one's cash position is different from the occurrence of sales and expenses: As an author, I process all receipts and expenses related to my writing through a separate checking account. (I maintain this separate account for tax reasons—just in case Uncle Sam ever wants to audit my records.) Although I receive a royalty each time one of my books is sold, it would be practically impossible for the publisher to send me a royalty check each time this happens. Instead, my publisher monitors sales, and twice a year I receive a check for the books that have been sold in recent months. In the meantime, though, I must pay my writing expenses. And although I'm quite interested in how my books are selling in the stores, it is the money in my checking account that pays my bills. The sales activity and my checking account balance are related in the long run, but I know all too well that they certainly are not one and the same thing.

The pro forma income statement and pro forma balance sheet are fairly straightforward. As you might guess, the pro forma income statement anticipates sales, expenses, and earnings over a given period of time. The pro forma balance sheet gives the expected picture of the company at a given time in the future.

Many good books can teach you the fine points of preparing financial projections; I've listed several in the Bibliography. To succeed with your banker, however, you do need to have an overview of what financial projections contain and how they are reviewed by a banker.

That's coming up in Chapter 6.

CHAPTER 6

Looking Ahead: Financial Projections Made Easy

The easiest place to start when preparing financial projections is with the projected income statement. Next, figure out the cash budget, and, finally, complete the projected balance sheet.

Pro Forma (Projected) Income Statement

You can prepare a projected income statement, usually called a *pro forma income statement,* for any period of time. It can be for a single business cycle or cover several years. Most often, business owners and accountants prepare these statements for a one-year period, the company's annual accounting period. In financial circles, the term used to describe this annual accounting period is the *fiscal year.*

The pro forma income statement is a best guess of what sales, expenses, and profits will be during the year. Thus, it makes sense to complete the projections before the fiscal year starts. That way, it's possible to compare actual results with the plan.

The first step is to project the level of sales for the fiscal year.

Sales Forecast

Consider several factors when projecting sales:

- Historic trends.
- Competition.
- Economic conditions.
- Factors unique to your company.

After assessing these factors, you will be able to estimate sales for the coming year. Once you have projected sales, your next step is to estimate expenses.

Expense Forecast

Expenses fall into three general categories: (1) cost of goods sold, (2) general and administrative expenses, and (3) other income and expenses.

With most businesses, the category of the cost of goods sold usually is a given percentage of the firm's sales. Let's say the cost of goods sold has averaged 35 percent of sales over the past few years. It would be logical to assume that during the coming year, the cost of goods sold also will be about 35 percent. Of course, many factors could cause this percentage to be different during the coming year, thus requiring you to adjust your expectations. For example, maybe you recently acquired equipment that will reduce manufacturing costs. Or perhaps you plan on doing a better job of controlling inventory or making some other improvement that you hope will increase profits.

The next step is to estimate the two remaining expense categories: general and administrative expenses and other revenues and expenses. Estimate these by looking at previous records, taking into account experience and expectations for the coming year. Subtracting all expenses from the revenues gives the anticipated profits.

To understand financial projections more easily, let's look at an example. Figure 6-1 is the pro forma income statement completed by Deborah Hoban, the president and owner of Hoban's Hardware, Inc., a wholesaler of building materials.

Figure 6-1. Hoban's Hardware, Inc., pro forma income statement.

HOBAN'S HARDWARE, INC.
Pro Forma Income Statement
($ in 000s)

	Actual 19X2	**%**	**Projected 19X3**	**%**
Sales	$3,300	100.0%	$3,600	100.0%
Cost of goods sold	2,385	72.3	2,600	72.2
Gross profit	915	27.7	1,000	27.8
General and administrative expenses	814		876	
Depreciation	26		24	
Total	840	25.5	900	25.0
Operating profit	75	2.3	100	2.8
Other income (expense)	(5)		(10)	
Before-tax profit	70	2.1	90	2.5
Taxes	8		12	
Net profit	$ 62	1.9%	$ 78	2.2%

Deborah has decided to project sales at $3,600,000 in 19X3, an increase of 9 percent over the previous year. She feels this is a realistic goal based on the historical trend and the status of the industry. Also, her company has hired a new sales representative, which will increase the sales level.

The next step is to look at expenses. Cost of goods sold is the first category. Deborah knows that in recent years, the cost of goods sold has averaged just over 72 percent. Therefore in 19X3, she projects the cost of goods sold to be $2,600,000. This figure amounts to 72.2 percent of sales for the projected year.

Subtracting the cost of goods sold from the sales gives the gross profit. Then she subtracts the general and administrative expenses and other income and expenses.

After reviewing the general and administrative expenses, Deborah is convinced that she can reduce certain expenses. She plans to cut back the general and administrative expenses as a percentage of sales. In the coming year, operating expenses are projected at 25 percent of sales as compared to 25.5 percent in 19X2.

Subtracting all expenses from sales shows Deborah estimates pretax profits will be $90,000. This is much better than $70,000 earned the previous year. She projects her net profit margin ratio at 2.5 percent, up from last year's 2.1 percent.

Upon completing the pro forma income statement, her next step is to prepare the cash budget.

The Cash Budget

A cash budget should supply the answers to four important questions:

1. How much money is needed from the bank?
2. When is it needed?
3. How will it be repaid?
4. When will the bank be repaid?

A cash budget describes the borrowing needs of a business over time. It outlines on paper those activities that will cause a change in a company's cash position.

A cash budget can never be totally accurate, but having approximate answers to these questions is a great aid in estimating financial needs. It is also a great aid in selling bankers on the merits of your business venture. After completing a cash budget, you will know and understand your monetary needs. The budget allows you more time to spend running your business since you won't have to be reacting to one financial crisis after another.

The five steps in preparing a cash budget are as follows:

Step 1: Break down the pro forma income statement into monthly revenues and expenses. Looking at the previous years' monthly pattern of sales and expenses is the best way to determine monthly figures. For most businesses, the percentage of sales in any month is fairly consistent from one year to the next. For example, the owner of a bookstore located in a ski resort knows that January and February will be busy times. During the summer doldrums, when the resort is empty, he probably won't make enough profit to buy a cup of coffee.

Step 2: Analyze accounts receivable and accounts payable. Sales and expense activity is not the same as cash activity because often cash is not received at the time of a sale. In addition, payments to suppliers are usually made a month or so after receiving the goods. If you review the historic time lag that occurs before payments are received and suppliers are paid, you can make any necessary adjustments.

Step 3: Estimate normal and routine expenses. Most expenses fall into either cost of goods sold or general and administrative expenses. At times, estimating the cost of goods sold each month can be a little tricky. The reason is that some expenses are paid during the month, and others are not. For example, employees who produce the goods might get a weekly paycheck. Yet invoices for materials might sit a month or so before being paid.

Each company and each industry is a little different, but looking at past results allows you to make accurate projections.

Kathleen Sullivan is the owner of a chain of restaurants, appropriately named Kathleen's Kitchen. Over the past four years, her cost of goods sold as a percentage of sales has averaged 40.2, 39.7, 40.6, and 40.1 percent. Using this historic information, she estimates her cost of goods sold at 40.0 percent of sales during the coming year.

Most costs in the general and administrative category are paid on a monthly basis. Rent is a good example of a recurring monthly expense. Therefore, when you prepare a cash budget, it's often easiest to divide the total annual cost by 12 (the 12 months to the year). You can then use this figure as the monthly cash expense. If you want a more detailed estimate of expenses, the best way to figure that is to look at historic trends and then make necessary adjustments.

Ryan Patrick, a surgeon, estimates that his general and administrative expense will be $180,000 in the coming year. From experience, he knows that his expenses are roughly the same each month. So he divides this figure by 12 to obtain a general and administrative monthly expense of $15,000 ($180,000 divided by 12).

Step 4: Forecast unusual or nonrecurring receipts and expenditures. You need to incorporate into your plan all atypical revenues and disbursements. For example, maybe you will acquire a piece of equipment during the year. Or perhaps you will receive a sizable sum of money from the settlement of a legal suit. Such activities would obviously change the company's cash position.

Step 5: Record changes in the cash position on a monthly basis. The next step is to incorporate your information, one month at a time. Start with a beginning cash balance for the month. Then record activities that either add to or subtract from your business's cash position. The result is the ending cash position for the month, which becomes the beginning balance for the next month.

The formula for noting changes can be stated as follows:

Beginning cash position
\+ Cash received during month
− Cash paid during month

= Ending cash position

In the past Deborah Hoban has borrowed money from the bank. Before she approaches her lending officer, she needs to know her financial needs so she can explain to the banker how much money she needs and when she needs it. She also must know how and when she will repay the banker. Her cash budget provides this information.

Let's review the steps taken by the owner of Hoban's Hardware to complete her cash budget.

Hoban's Hardware's Cash Budget

Deborah starts with certain assumptions. They are:

1. Sales for the company (in thousands) will be as follows during the coming year:

Month	*Percentage*	*Amount*
January	3.0	$ 108
February	3.0	108
March	4.0	144
April	5.0	180
May	10.0	360
June	20.0	720
July	20.0	720
August	20.0	720
September	5.0	180
October	4.0	144
November	3.0	108
December	3.0	108
	100.0	$3,600

2. Accounts receivable will be collected 30 days after the date of sale.
3. The cost of goods sold category consists mainly of the payroll and expenses of materials purchased. The payroll expense will be spread evenly over the year. Suppliers will be paid the month after the company receives the materials.
4. Operating expenses will be evenly disbursed over the year.
5. An adjustment in inventory levels, equipment purchase, and miscellaneous expense will affect the cash position during the summer months.
6. The cash balance will be $10,000 or more at all times.

Deborah Hoban breaks down the pro forma income statement into monthly segments, as shown in Figure 6-2.

You'll notice Deborah separated depreciation (the write-off of an asset's useful life over time) from the other general and administrative expenses. Depreciation is referred to as a noncash expense because it doesn't take any cash out of the company. It is simply subtracted as an expense on the income statement for tax purposes.

After dividing the pro forma income statement into monthly figures, the next step is to determine the cash budget.

The cash budget for Hoban's Hardware is the second part of Figure 6-2. The beginning cash position in January for the firm is $85,000. During the month, Deborah Hoban will need to borrow $32,000 from the bank to maintain her desired minimum cash position of $10,000.

She repeats the process for February and each of the following months during the year. Upon completing the plan, Deborah will know her borrowing needs for the coming year. Because much of her company's business occurs in the summer, she must start borrowing in January. Her cash needs peak during early summer. It is expected that she can repay the bank in full by early fall. She expects to borrow the most in May.

Her cash budget for Hoban's might not prove to be accurate. Considering this reality, Deborah might ask to borrow a maximum amount of $425,000 or $450,000. That way, she would have money available in case her cash budget misses the mark.

Now put yourself in the shoes of Deborah's banker. If she approached you with such a well-thought-out and detailed cash budget, wouldn't you be impressed? Of course you would. It's obvious the owner of Hoban's is planning ahead rather than reacting to one financial crisis after another. She knows and understands the financial needs of her company.

Business owners should present their cash budgets to bankers well in advance of the date when their firms actually need the money. This allows the bankers plenty of time to present borrowing requests to loan committees for approval. The loan approval process takes time. Depending on the bank and the amount desired by the borrower, the process can take from a couple of days to two weeks—sometimes even longer.

You can imagine the problems that can develop if an owner waits until the last minute to ask for the needed funds. If loan

Figure 6-2. Hoban's Hardware, Inc., monthly pro forma income statement and cash budget.

HOBAN'S HARDWARE, INC.
Monthly Pro Forma Income Statement and Cash Budget
19X3
($ in 000s)

	Jan	Feb	Mar	Apr	May	Jun	Jul	Aug	Sep	Oct	Nov	Dec	Total
Sales	108	108	144	180	360	720	720	720	180	144	108	108	3,600
Cost of goods sold	78	78	104	130	260	520	520	520	130	104	78	78	2,600
Gross profit	30	30	40	50	100	200	200	200	50	40	30	30	1,000
Operating expenses	73	73	73	73	73	73	73	73	73	73	73	73	876
Depreciation	2	2	2	2	2	2	2	2	2	2	2	2	24
Total	75	75	75	75	75	75	75	75	75	75	75	75	900
Operating profit	(45)	(45)	(35)	(25)	25	125	125	125	(25)	(35)	(45)	(45)	100
Other income (expense)							(10)						(10)
Net profit before taxes	(45)	(45)	(35)	(25)	25	125	115	125	(25)	(35)	(45)	(45)	90

CASH BUDGET

Cash balance beginning	85	10	10	10	10	10	10	10	87	354	291	206
Plus receipts												
Accounts receivable collected	108	108	108	144	180	360	720	720	720	180	144	108
Bank loan required	32	107	107	85	83							
Total cash available	225	225	225	239	273	370	730	730	807	534	435	314
Less disbursements												
Raw materials	42	42	42	56	70	140	280	280	280	70	56	42
Payroll	100	100	100	100	100	100	100	100	100	100	100	100
General and administrative expenses	73	73	73	73	73	73	73	73	73	73	73	73
Base inventory increase					20	20	10	10				
Equipment							40					
Other							10					
Bank loan repaid						27	207	180				
Total disbursements	215	215	215	229	263	360	720	643	453	243	229	215
Cash balance ending	10	10	10	10	10	10	10	87	354	291	206	99
Cumulative bank loan	32	139	246	331	414	387	180					

Figure 6-3. Hoban's Hardware, Inc., pro forma balance sheet.

HOBAN'S HARDWARE, INC.
Balance Sheet
($ in 000s)

	Actual 19X2	Pro Forma 19X3
ASSETS		
Cash	$ 85	$ 110
Accounts receivable	350	400
Inventory	580	650
Prepaid expenses	85	110
Total current assets	$1,100	$1,270
Net fixed assets	210	230
Other assets	100	125
TOTAL ASSETS	$1,410	$1,625
LIABILITIES		
Accounts payable	$ 300	$ 325
Other current liabilities	440	554
Total current liabilities	740	879
Long-term liabilities	90	88
TOTAL LIABILITIES	$ 830	$ 967
Net worth	$ 580	$ 658
TOTAL NET WORTH AND LIABILITIES	$1,410	$1,625

approval is declined—or even delayed—the company would run out of cash.

Of the three financial projections, the cash budget is the most important, especially from the banker's perspective. In addition to the pro forma income statement and the cash budget, sometimes bankers also want a projected balance sheet.

Pro Forma (Projected) Balance Sheet

The final step after completing the pro forma income statement and the cash budget is preparation of the pro forma balance sheet.

The pro forma balance sheet is an estimate of what a company is going to look like at a given time in the future. The balance sheet and income statement are interrelated. Since they work together, the sales activity is going to change what is owned by the company and what the company owes to others.

I like to think of the projected balance sheet as a reflection of a company's future sales. As the level of sales increases, so must the need for assets. Because the balance sheet and sales forecast are so closely connected, it is possible to construct the pro forma balance sheet as soon as the sales forecast is completed. Once you have a good idea where sales are headed, you can estimate the level of assets and liabilities you'll need.

As a company's sales go up, it is usually necessary to have a higher cash position. Along with the rise in sales, accounts receivable, inventory, and trade payables also increase. Other assets and liabilities may or may not change. If the equipment is adequate to handle increased sales activity, it may not be necessary to purchase any new equipment. The same applies to the company's plant and facilities. They may or may not be adequate to handle the increased sales level.

Hoban's Hardware balance sheet for 19X2 and the pro forma balance sheet for the following year are shown in Figure 6-3.

Deborah Hoban has identified certain items on the balance sheet that historically have fluctuated with sales. She calculates the relationship of these items to sales using the following equation:

$$\frac{\text{Asset or liability}}{\text{Sales}} = \text{Percentage}$$

For 19X2 Deborah made these calculations:

$$\frac{\text{Cash}}{\text{Sales}} = \frac{\$85}{\$3{,}300} = 3.0\%$$

$$\frac{\text{Accounts receivable}}{\text{Sales}} = \frac{\$350}{\$3{,}300} = 11.0\%$$

$$\frac{\text{Inventory}}{\text{Sales}} = \frac{\$580}{\$3{,}300} = 18.0\%$$

$$\frac{\text{Prepaid expenses}}{\text{Sales}} = \frac{\$85}{\$3{,}300} = 3.0\%$$

$$\frac{\text{Accounts payable}}{\text{Sales}} = \frac{\$300}{\$3{,}300} = 9.0\%$$

By assuming that the relationship between these balance sheet items and sales will continue in the future, Deborah has projected the following for 19X3.

Item	*Percentage of Sales*		*19X3 Sales Forecast*		*12-31-X3 Balance*
Cash	3.0	×	$3,600	=	$108
Accounts receivable	11.0	×	$3,600	=	$396
Inventory	18.0	×	$3,600	=	$648
Prepaid expenses	3.0	×	$3,600	=	$108
Accounts payable	9.0	×	$3,600	=	$324

Deborah's next step is to calculate the net worth for 12-31-X3 by adding the after-tax profit for 19X3 to the net worth in 19X2:

Old Net Worth	+	*After-Tax Profit*	=	*Pro Forma Net Worth*
$580	+	$78	=	$658

Using these data—and some common sense—she "guesstimates" the remaining items on the balance sheet. Since assets need to equal liabilities and net worth, she makes adjustments so that the two sides of the balance sheet are equal.

How Far Do You Miss the Mark?

A plan is only a plan. It might prove to be accurate or miss the mark by a mile. Accuracy in numbers, however, isn't as important as knowing and understanding why there is a discrepancy.

Maybe the company received a large order that wasn't expected. Perhaps severe weather hampered business. Or maybe the competition opened an outlet across the street. All of these are explanations for discrepancies. When running a business, it's important to understand and—when possible—predict the impact such events have on the business.

To make a plan and then not refer to it regularly defeats its purpose. Some entrepreneurs like to review results quarterly. Others prefer to make comparisons more frequently, such as monthly or biweekly. They discuss deviations from the plan with key employees and decide on corrective action. Sometimes they adjust the plan to reflect reality better.

Financial planning isn't difficult. It just takes a little time and effort. If you want to successfully borrow a large amount of money from a bank, you must plan your finances so both you and your banker can use this information.

Plan for Your Success

I know of many cases in which financial planning was the key ingredient in turning around a marginally profitable operation. This is because financial planning charts the course for a company. It outlines in quantifiable terms where you are now and where you want to be. Once objectives are set, you can allocate the resources and manpower necessary to reach your goals—like a pilot navigating an airplane toward a destination. The pilot knows where he's going. It's just a matter of making occasional adjustments to maintain the course. Financial planning operates in the same way.

Over the years Fritz Ribary has owned and successfully operated many businesses—everything from a limousine service to a silver mine. Fritz's specialty is buying companies that are mismanaged, turning around their profit situation, and selling them for a tidy profit.

When he buys a company, one of Fritz's first steps is to sit down with the members of his management team and outline on paper the company's financial future. "You need to know where you're headed. Otherwise you're like a ship without a rudder," Fritz once said to me. "Most small businessmen don't take the time to plan their company's financial future. They use the excuse that they are too busy fighting brushfires. But I think they are wrong. Planning is the difference between you running your business and your business running you."

No wonder he is successful.

CHAPTER 7

Types of Business Loans

Upon completing financial projections, most business people realize that they will need to borrow money from a bank. Before approaching a banker for a loan, you should know exactly what kinds of loans a banker makes. In this chapter, I'll discuss the four types of business loans made by bankers and in Chapter 8 explain how each of these loans is normally repaid.

Commercial banks usually classify their business loans into four types: business cycle loan, working capital loan, term loan, and interim loan. Each is geared to meet a different kind of financing need. Based on the information presented by a business owner, a banker will think in terms of one particular type of loan.

Let's review them one at a time.

Business Cycle Loans

All companies have a business trading cycle. The cycle starts when companies have cash. The owner uses this cash to offer goods or services to the marketplace. The cycle is complete when customers replenish the company's cash by paying for the goods and/or services.

A business trading cycle for a manufacturer is illustrated in Figure 7-1.

Figure 7-1. Business trading cycle.

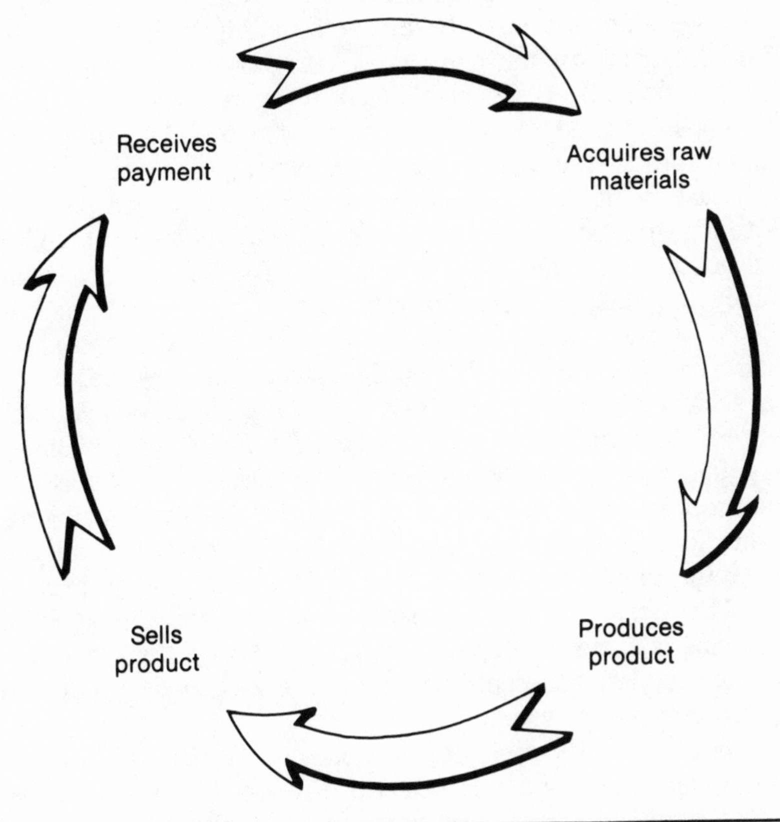

The cycle starts with cash and, upon completion, ends with the collection of cash from customers. Various factors affect a company's business cycle. Patterson's Foundry, Inc., purchased a new induction melting furnace and linear accelerator that shortened production time from 13 days to 8 days. This shortened Patterson's business cycle accordingly.

In comparison, Worthington's Framing, a framing contractor, usually collects accounts receivable in about 30 days. Due to a recent slowdown in the economy, however, Worthington's collection period now is running about 45 days. Not only that, but some customers appear unlikely to be able to pay the firm at all. Because of this situation, Worthington's business trading cycle has been lengthened.

It's easy to see how the business trading cycle has a substantial impact on the company's cash position. In turn, the cash position affects the firm's need to borrow money.

Let's examine the business cycles of two other companies. Nancy Jordan, the owner of a downtown espresso stand, starts with cash, which she uses to buy espresso beans and pastries. Within a few hours, her customers have purchased the coffee and goodies, and the cycle is compete. The business cycle for Nancy's espresso company is very short.

Most other firms do not have such a rapid turnover of their inventory. Dennis Newell, the owner of a toy store, stocks his shelves during the early fall. There are about two months between the time when the shelves are full and when customers buy the toys as Christmas presents. Unless Dennis has the resources to cover this period of time, he will need financing. Either toy suppliers say, "You don't have to pay me until you make the sale," or Dennis will need financing to pay them.

The type of loan requested to assist with this type of financing is a *business cycle loan.* It helps bridge the gap in the business cycle—between when money needs to be spent and before cash is recovered.

With business cycle loans, business owners can request money for a variety of reasons—to increase their inventory, to meet payroll, or to assist with marketing and selling the products. Regardless of the need, this type of loan is always repaid by the end of the business cycle.

Usually the need for business cycle financing arises from an anticipated increase in sales. Money from the bank helps meet the expenses associated with this increased activity.

Generally business cycle loans constitute a fairly low risk to the bank because typically the debt is repaid within a short period of time.

Working Capital Loans

Bankers and accountants define *working capital* as follows:

Current assets − Current liabilities = Working capital

Current assets are assets the owner expects to be converted into cash within the coming year. Accounts receivable and inventory are examples. Current liabilities are debts to be paid in the coming year, for example, bills from suppliers. If a company's current assets are $100,000 and current liabilities are $60,000, the working capital is $40,000 ($100,000 – $60,000 = $40,000).

The relationship between current assets and current liabilities is important, since it reflects a company's ability to pay its bills in the near future. Sometimes a banker looks at a company's solvency by checking the working capital. Other times the banker will look at the current ratio (current assets divided by current liabilities). Both measure solvency, but each from a different perspective.

The amount of working capital a company needs depends to a large degree on the type of industry it is in. Manufacturers need a large amount of working capital because they have a large amount of money invested in inventory and accounts receivable. Also, their business cycle is much longer than that of other types of industries. A manufacturer starts with cash, produces the product, sells it, and then has to wait for the money.

Wholesalers and retailers need less working capital than manufacturers because they do not have a production phase in their business cycles. Like Dennis, the toy store owner, however, all retailers and wholesalers do have inventory, which sits on the shelf for a period of time.

As you might expect, service companies need far less working capital than manufacturers, wholesalers, or retailers since service companies do not need to invest money either in making a product or stocking inventory. In fact, public utilities often have more current liabilities than they have current assets. This gives them a negative working capital position.

The working capital loan is similar to the business cycle loan but with an important difference. By requesting a working capital loan, a business owner is acknowledging a permanent need for more working capital. Business cycle loans, by contrast, are designed to meet a temporary need.

Business owners use working capital loans to increase current assets or reduce current liabilities. Here are two examples. Kurt Olsen, a men's clothing retailer, is going to expand and wants to increase his level of inventory. Since inventory is a current asset and his need is permanent rather than temporary, his request will fall in the working capital category. Eileen Quackenbush, owner of a jewelry store, asks her banker for a loan to pay off a major supplier. She plans to repay the loan over a two-year period. Since she is asking for money to decrease her company's current liabilities, her request also falls in the working capital loan category.

As expected, manufacturers usually have the greatest need for working capital loans, followed by wholesalers, retailers, and, last, service companies.

For the bank, the longer repayment period of the working capital loan creates more uncertainty and risk, because it's easier to predict the financial affairs of a company in the near future than to estimate what will happen several years down the road.

Term Loans

Term loans are different from the other loans we've discussed. They are generally used to finance the acquisition of a non-current asset, such as equipment, fixtures, or facilities. Non-current assets are anything a company owns that probably won't be converted into cash in the near future.

Patricia Gerrard, owner of Gerrard Insurance Agency, has decided to purchase a new IBM computer system for her office. The cost of the system is $20,000. Although she needs the new computer, she doesn't want to deplete her cash position, so she has decided to approach her banker for a term loan. He agrees to lend her $15,000, secured by the computer, and Patricia is paying the bank $487 each month over three years.

This is a typical example of a term loan. Although term loans are usually used to acquire physical assets, this isn't always the case. For example, an entrepreneur may request money to assist with expenses associated with product development.

Term loans are a higher risk to the bank than working capital loans and business cycle loans. This is because the time frame required to repay the bank is longer than that used with the other types of loans.

Interim Loans

Interim loans are less common than the other types we've discussed. With interim loans, the bank officer is concerned with *how* the money will be repaid. Unlike the other three types of financing, *why* the money is requested is of less importance to the banker. By definition, with interim loans, the bank will be repaid from one of two sources: by another creditor or by the owner's putting more money into the company from his or her personal resources.

Let's say Ed Kleffner, a fiberglass boat manufacturer, wants to build a new warehouse. Ed wants to be the general contractor for the project. It's important to him to coordinate the construction phase and pay the subcontractors, so he approaches his bank for a loan. Ed tells his banker that upon completion of his warehouse, a long-term loan from a mortgage company will be used to repay the bank. Since Ed's repayment source is another creditor, the bank will classify his financing as an interim loan.

The Bottom Line: Obtaining the Right Kind of Loan

When you approach a banker for a loan, it's important that you know—and be able to explain—your financing needs. Being able to give tangible and specific reasons as to why you need the money and how it will be spent is essential.

A loan for a couple of months to increase your inventory is a much different type of financing need from borrowing to buy a new corporate jet. A different type of loan is required.

Being able to tell your banker what kind of loan you need—a business cycle, working capital, term, or interim loan—shows that you understand your financial situation. Having the same perspective, you'll be working together toward solving your financing need.

CHAPTER 8

Right and Wrong Ways to Repay a Bank

Is there a wrong way to repay the bank? Surprisingly, the answer is yes—as far as you, the business owner, are concerned. (Bankers are happy with any repayment plan that delivers the money as promised.)

There are many different ways to repay the bank. Making payments to the bank from company's profit, by selling the furniture in the lunchroom, or by borrowing money from another bank down the street are all possibilities. Indeed, the options are practically endless.

When you are thinking about structuring a repayment plan, you should remember this basic rule: *When you pay back the bank is based on* why *you are borrowing the money. The repayment period needs to coincide with the reason for the financing request.*

In other words, how you as a business owner use the loan money has a definite impact on when your company will have enough cash to repay the bank. Remember Dennis Newell, the toy store owner who needed to borrow money to increase his pre-Christmas inventory? Assuming Dennis has a good holiday season, he'll be in good shape to repay the bank in January. If Dennis were borrowing to expand his store, however, a different type of repayment program would make sense. In this case, Dennis is making an investment in his firm that will generate money over many years. As such, it's logical for him to make monthly payments to the bank over several years.

A loan request for short-term needs should be repaid in the short term. Loan requests for long-term needs should be paid back over a longer period of time.

Randy Carter runs a nursery and needs to increase his inventory of plants, flowers, and other gardening supplies in the early spring. He needs to borrow money from his banker to buy all this merchandise. During the late spring and early summer, the inventory gradually will be converted into cash. Once the peak selling season is over, it makes sense for him to repay the loan to the bank. Randy usually pays back the bank in late July or early August.

Last year, however, Randy decided to buy and install a state-of-the-art computer system that will keep track of his inventory and sales activity. Buying the computer system was to meet a long-term need. Randy and his banker agreed it would make sense for him to repay the bank over a two-year period.

Is the Repayment Plan Logical?

When listening to a borrowing request, the typical banker focuses on two questions. Is the loan request logical, and does the proposed repayment plan make sense? If the reasons for the loan and the repayment plan seem reasonable, the banker is likely to give thumbs up. If either of these factors does not make sense to the loan officer, he will decline the request.

I remember an entrepreneur who came into my bank and requested a sizable amount of money to buy some new equipment. Buying the equipment made sense. But he said that he intended to repay the bank in 90 days. I thought it extremely unlikely that his firm would have enough money to repay the bank in such a short time, so I asked, "How in the world did you come up with a 90-day repayment period?"

The customer told me that his neighbor was a successful businessman who frequently borrowed from his banker. He always repaid his loans in 90 days. Taking his neighbor's example, my customer thought it was proper protocol to request a 90-day loan.

This poor man was requesting a plan that was not in his best interests. There was no way that his firm would have enough cash to repay my bank in 90 days. In three months, faced with a huge payment, what was he going to do? Come back into my bank and ask for another 90-day loan? (This story has a happy ending. Once I fully understood his financial situation I approved his loan—with a four-year repayment schedule.)

What Happens If Your Plans Don't Work?

A banker always wants to know how a borrower will repay the loan. Often he won't be satisfied with your initial answer to the repayment query and will press for more details: "What will you do if that doesn't happen? Then how are you going to repay the bank?" To say that bankers are cautious is an understatement. They constantly play the game of "what if?" and don't focus their energy on the good news. They are concerned with how you will meet your loan payments if the bottom falls out of your business. Typically bankers get more points with their bosses for not making mistakes—for not making bad loans—than when they bring in new business. So this skepticism—some might say an unrelenting pessimistic viewpoint—is rewarded by superiors.

Bankers are trained to look for a primary and secondary repayment source for every business loan. The way you intend to repay the loan is the *primary repayment source.* The backup method, or alternative means that can be used if your plans don't work out as expected, is commonly referred to as the *secondary repayment source.* Bankers have learned over the years that when borrowers have two separate means of repaying the debt, the likelihood of a loss is substantially reduced.

Consider what happens when you apply for a home mortgage. Both you and the lender hope that your monthly income will be sufficient to make the monthly house payments. The lender looks at your employment history, income, and expenses in deciding whether to grant your loan request. However, the cold hard reality is that if for some reason the payments are not made, the mortgage banker still wants the money. To ensure payment, the bank takes a lien against your property for its protection when the loan is made. If necessary, the bank will foreclose on the property and use the proceeds from the sale to pay off the mortgage. In this example, your monthly income is the primary repayment source. The house represents the secondary repayment source.

The Art of Repaying Business Loans

Business Cycle Loans

When presented with a business cycle loan request, a banker starts by looking at the company's business cycle. Reviewing the cycle with a business owner usually points to *when* and *why* the company needs the money.

The next step is to determine when the current assets will convert into cash. In banking circles, the term used to describe this process is *asset conversion.* The best tool to understand this situation is the cash budget. It outlines on paper how much and when the money is needed. It also shows how and when the bank will be repaid.

Typically a business cycle loan represents a low risk for the bank because usually it is designed with a short repayment period. But what happens if the company doesn't do the business anticipated? Bill Taylor, a commercial fisherman, borrows to meet expenses for his fishing season. Due to poor weather, he doesn't catch what he expects. At the end of the season, he doesn't have the cash to repay the bank. Bill is washed up.

Sad to say, but Bill's options and his banker's choices are limited:

- If Bill has a good track record, his banker will extend the loan for a longer period of time, betting that Bill will recoup his losses with the next fishing season (and hoping that Mother Nature cooperates with good weather).
- If Bill's past performance doesn't inspire confidence, the banker will ask Bill to sell his assets to repay the loan.

> The loan officer will review Bill's financial statement to evaluate which assets (stocks, the boat, his house, and anything else) he might sell. In the worst-case scenario, Bill would have to sell his boat to repay the loan, which would put him out of business.

Working Capital and Term Loans

Working capital and term loans have the same primary source of repayment: the future profits of a company, as described in the firm's pro forma income statement.

The usual repayment period for working capital and term loans ranges from one to seven years. With loans secured by real estate, the repayment period is longer.

With these types of loans, usually a borrower makes monthly payments to the bank. Sometimes it makes more sense for a company to make payments every three months, yearly, or on some other schedule. It depends on the company. Farmers and fishermen, for example, probably will make an annual payment after selling their products.

Since earnings can be difficult to estimate, bankers often ask some probing questions. Is the owner intending on buying any other major pieces of equipment? Is the working capital position expected to grow? If so, by how much, as this would affect the company's cash position? What other payments need to be made to other creditors? A banker wants to be sure there will be enough cash to make the payments to the bank. Sometimes a banker looks to the company's pro forma balance sheet for some of these answers.

To a banker, uncertainty is the same as risk. A banker faced with uncertainty (a loan that will be repaid over many months or years) will request collateral. If you run into problems, the cash from the sale of the collateral will repay the bank.

Bankers want business owners, not the bank's depositors, to take the risk.

Interim Loans

By definition, interim loans are repaid from one of two sources: the creditor paying off the bank or the owner putting more money into the company.

Table 8-1. Repayment sources for business loans.

Type of Business Loan	*Primary Source of Repayment*	*Financial Projections Reviewed*	*Secondary Sources of Repayment*	*Financial Projections Reviewed*
Business cycle loan	Asset conversion	Cash budget	Profits Other creditors Owner's capital	Pro forma income statement Pro forma balance sheet
Working capital loan	Profits	Pro forma income statement Pro forma balance sheet	Asset conversion Other creditors Owner's capital	Cash budget
Term loan	Profits	Pro forma income statement Pro forma balance sheet	Asset conversion Other creditors Owner's capital	Cash budget
Interim	Other creditors Owner's capital		Profits	Pro forma income statement Pro forma balance sheet
			Asset conversion	Cash budget

When looking at an interim loan request, a banker focuses primarily on whether the commitment is sound. Of course, sometimes commitments do not materialize as expected, so the banker will also look at the overall financial strength and outlook for the company to determine whether the company can repay the bank if something happens to the primary repayment source. Usually this would be by:

- The company's profits
- The company selling assets
- The owner's personal financial resources

The Bottom Line: Repaying the Bank

How you repay the bank has a major impact on your company's cash flow. A proper repayment program is as important as being able to obtain financing in the first place.

When discussing repayment options with your banker, always remember that the repayment schedule should depend on why you are borrowing the money. The length of time needed to repay the debt depends on how the money will be spent.

Table 8-1 summarizes the four business loan types and how they are usually repaid.

Now that you know what kind of business loans bankers make and how these loans are normally repaid, I'm going to explain what lending guidelines a banker considers when reviewing your request.

CHAPTER 9

The Banker's Bible: Lending Guidelines

Good bankers can look at a situation, perceive the essential facts, and reach logical conclusions. A banker listening to a request for money is always asking himself, "Does this make sense?" Before lending a thin dime, a banker wants assurances that the entrepreneur is looking at the situation realistically rather than just chasing a pot of gold at the end of the rainbow.

Let's look at one man's story.

John Horton worked for the post office as a mail carrier. He had the same job for 14 years. John and his family lived from paycheck to paycheck. Like many other people, the Hortons had no money left over at the end of the month. One evening, John and his wife, Abby, attended a motivational seminar on the benefits of investing in real estate. It was one of these programs where the speaker promises that if you do exactly what he says, you'll get rich. (I like to call those programs "how to get rich by a week from Friday or sooner.")

After attending the program, John and Abby wanted to buy a fixer-upper house in their neighborhood. They intended to upgrade the residence and then resell it for a tidy profit. When John approached me at the bank, he was full of enthusiasm. He thought he could buy the property for $45,000 and spend only about $5,000 to repair it. John estimated that by reducing the number of hours he worked at the post office, he could complete the improvements within a couple of months, sell the property, and pocket a profit of about $10,000.

He approached me because he wanted to borrow $50,000 (the purchase price of the house plus the cost of improvements). In my opinion, John and Abby were just wishful thinkers. "What ifs" flooded my brain. What if John underestimated the cost of repairs? What if the property sat vacant for a number of months? How would John and Abby be able to pay their living expenses if he reduced the number of hours he worked at the post office? (Abby's part-time job paid for only a small percentage of their monthly living expenses.) The list of my potential concerns went on and on. True, if everything went according to the plan, the couple would make a nice profit. But that was a very big if. It was an enormous risk my bank was not willing to take.

Banks Don't Lose—Much

Bankers are in business to lend money and get it repaid—with interest. That's their number-one priority. When speaking on the topic of banking, I sometimes open my presentation by asking: "What percentage of a bank's loans are losses due to customers' not paying?" The answers from the audience vary considerably. Most people guess it's somewhere between 10 and 30 percent.

Well, it's *much* lower than that. Banks get their loan money repaid nearly all of the time. A bank's charge-off rate (or what I call their mistake rate) is low. For most banks it is about 1.5 percent. In other words, 98.5 percent of the time, banks are repaid. Unless bankers are extremely confident that would-be borrowers can repay the bank, the money does not leave the vault.

Of course, the 1.5 percent represents actual losses. Entrepreneurs may have cash flow problems, but the bank eventually gets its money when the borrower's assets are sold. It's easy to figure that an error rate under 2 percent doesn't allow much room for error. When I was a junior lending officer, I turned down the loan request of a man; let's call him Clyde. I decided against the loan because his credit history showed that he was extremely slow in paying his bills. During our discussion, Clyde blamed his financial problems on his ex-wife's irresponsible habits. In fact, he said that she ran off with her gynecologist.

I wasn't convinced that his ex-wife was the cause of the problems. Despite my clear refusal to okay the loan, Clyde was the type who wouldn't take no for an answer. The next day, he made an appointment with my boss and again presented his request. This time he added that I was a typical banker: stuffy, stodgy, and stubborn.

My boss, as it turned out, was also recently divorced. He decided to override my decision. Feeling sympathetic, he wanted to give Clyde a second chance. His emotions influenced his decision since he could relate so easily to the hurt and pain Clyde suffered in his divorce.

Unfortunately for the bank—and for my boss—Clyde never repaid the loan. In fact, he didn't make a single payment. My boss quickly went back to his usual method of evaluating loan requests: taking a good look at the numbers and the borrower's history.

Take a lesson from Clyde and remember these crucial lending guidelines:

1. Your loan request must make sense.
2. As a borrower, you must identify your primary and secondary means of repayment.
3. Your banker must be confident that the loan will be repaid.

Bankers Prefer Partial Financing

Bankers prefer to finance a portion of any project or endeavor rather than the entire amount. Let's say you are buying a new piece of equipment for $20,000. The bank wants you to come up with 25 percent ($5,000) of the acquisition cost. Then it will finance the balance.

Bankers like partial financing for three important reasons. First, bankers believe that when you put some of your own money into the project, you'll work harder to make the venture successful. It's obvious that the more you have invested, the more you have to lose.

Second, bankers are trying to minimize their risk and potential losses. In this example, it's probable that the banker would take a lien against the equipment and use it as collateral. If you were not able to make the payments, the equipment would be repossessed and then sold. The proceeds from the sale would be used to repay the debt.

It's possible that the proceeds from the sale would amount to $15,000, or 75 percent of the original price, thus generating enough cash to pay off the bank. The probability that the used equipment would generate revenues of the acquisition price of $20,000 is unlikely. More likely, by lending the full amount, the bank runs the risk of a loss.

Third, bankers want to deal with people who are solvent. They want customers who have some liquid financial resources in case they run into rough financial waters.

Look at it from the banker's perspective: How would you feel if someone sat down at your desk and wanted some money for a business venture but didn't have any of his own money to put into the project? Perhaps you might ask yourself: What in the world is this guy going to do if his plans don't materialize as expected? The answer is obvious: Either he will have to close his doors or borrow more money. Even if he is able to borrow more money, his problems will not have disappeared. Now it's going to be even harder for him to make a profit, since his interest expense is higher.

Is Your Signature Enough?

Sometimes a banker lends money without requesting that an asset be pledged as collateral. This type of loan is called *unsecured.* Other times a banker requires the borrower to pledge an asset as collateral (a *secured* loan).

Unsecured Loans

When deciding if a loan should be unsecured or secured, a banker considers several factors. Unsecured loans are generally made when the following conditions exist:

- The borrower is financially strong relative to the amount of money being requested.
- The borrower shows a history of stable income.
- The borrower's expenses are not excessive in relation to income.
- The borrower has an excellent history of paying obligations on time.
- The borrower is viewed as being capable, cooperative, and trustworthy.
- The outlook for the borrower's company appears bright.
- The loan will be repaid within the next 12 months.

If, when evaluating these factors, a banker thinks the financing request represents little risk to the bank, he will process the loan without requiring collateral. If all of these conditions are not met—but the banker still wants to make the loan—he would request that acceptable collateral be pledged.

There are several benefits to borrowing money without pledging collateral. First, your assets are unencumbered; you are free to sell them or, if desired, pledge them as collateral for future loans. Borrowing on an unsecured basis gives business owners more financial freedom. And the interest rate for unsecured loans is usually lower than that for collateralized loans. Sounds strange? There are a couple of reasons for this practice. First, a banker views unsecured loans as being of low risk. Second, the banker's paperwork is minimal with unsecured loans; therefore, the bank's processing cost of making the loan is reduced.

Considering these factors, whenever possible you should negotiate to borrow without having to pledge collateral.

Secured Loans

Bankers make secured loans when borrowers don't qualify for unsecured loans. In other words, a borrower's financial strength and earnings records are adequate, so the banker decides to make the loan—with collateral provided.

The point at which a loan is determined to be secured is actually a subjective decision that varies from bank to bank and from banker to banker. For instance, if a borrower requests

$30,000, the banker may grant the loan and not require collateral. Should the same borrower ask for $50,000, the banker might ask for an asset to be pledged as security.

Whether a banker requires collateral is determined by the applicant's creditworthiness and the length of the repayment period. As a general rule, a banker will request collateral on any loan with a repayment period that is longer than one year because the longer period represents a higher risk to the bank.

If you borrow to acquire an asset, expect the banker to use the asset being purchased as collateral. For instance, should a contractor borrow money to buy a new backhoe, the loan officer will use the backhoe as collateral. It's possible to pledge any free-and-clear asset, but bankers usually look to the acquired asset.

Because many borrowers frequently have multiple borrowing needs, banks often provide both unsecured and secured loans to the same company. A business cycle loan of $35,000 might be unsecured. Yet on an additional $15,000 loan needed to purchase a new company car, the banker probably would use the car as collateral. The reason is that the car loan will be repaid over several years.

Sometimes it's more convenient for everyone if the banker gives a credit line instead of an outright loan.

Loan or Credit Line?

Sometimes business owners have frequent needs for cash. They borrow money and repay it soon. Then they have a need for more money. This type of borrowing activity results in a fair amount of red tape for both borrowers and bankers. A *credit line,* an arrangement by which a bank agrees to lend a borrower up to a given amount of money, is designed to cut down the paperwork for customers and bankers. It is beneficial for customers who have frequent and fluctuating financing needs.

A credit line is similar to a credit card. For instance, a bank might agree to set up a credit line for a business owner in the amount of $200,000. The credit line can be established on either an unsecured or a secured basis. Usually the credit line is valid for one year.

Many times accounts receivable and/or inventory is used as collateral for credit lines. How would this type of credit line work? Let's look at an example.

Henry Graves owns National Appliances, a wholesaler of small appliances. Henry's banker establishes a credit line for the company with an upper limit of $150,000. The banker agrees to lend an amount up to 75 percent of National Appliances' current accounts receivable and 50 percent of the company's inventory value.

When Henry needs money, he brings to the bank a document stating the current amount of his accounts receivable and inventory. Then the banker gives Henry a percentage of the amount pledged. For instance, if Henry pledged receivables of $100,000 and inventory of $80,000, the banker would loan his company $115,000 ($100,000 × 0.75 + $80,000 × 0.50).

As a guideline, a banker will lend 70 to 80 percent of the current value of a company's accounts receivable. With inventory, the percentage loaned is much less; 50 percent of the inventory's value is common.

Credit lines can be convenient and efficient for bankers and borrowers. Frequently a borrower doesn't even have to come into the bank on a regular basis. The business owner simply calls the bank and has money transferred from the credit line to the checking account or vice-versa. The bank benefits by a substantial reduction in paperwork, which reduces the cost of managing the loan.

The Need for Revolvement

A word of caution about business credit lines is necessary: Bankers frequently keep tabs on credit lines to see if the amount of money a company owes the bank is fluctuating. The term bankers use for these fluctuations is *revolvement.*

Here's an example. Computer Specialists, Inc., is a company that sells, installs, and services mainframe computers. The company established a $400,000 credit line pledging its accounts receivable as collateral. Over several months, the outstanding balance on the line fluctuated between $240,000 and $400,000. The initial balance was $380,000, then $305,000, $260,000, $334,000, $400,000, $292,000, $240,000, and finally $324,000.

Bankers like revolvement; it shows that a borrower has enough money to repay the bank. If the amount borrowed remains at or near the top of the line, a banker becomes concerned. For instance, if the line balance for Computer Specialists, Inc., fluctuated only between $390,000 and $400,000 for a period of time, the banker would start asking questions. Bankers worry that a customer with little revolvement may not have the financial resources to repay the debts. While this may not be true, it is one of the unwritten rules of banking.

If you decide to establish a credit line, make sure that the amount you owe the bank fluctuates significantly enough to keep your loan officer happy—even if you lower the outstanding balance of the line and then borrow it back a few days later.

Now that you understand how a banker evaluates a loan request, you're ready to tackle a loan proposal. In the next chapter, I explain how to write a proposal that favorably impresses your banker—and sends you on your way with your money.

CHAPTER 10

Writing a Successful Loan Proposal

("Successful" means that you get the money)

Before a banker can decide if the financial institution can lend you money, he or she wants quite a bit of information—preferably in writing. It is true that you can explain much of what the banker wants to know during the initial interview, but you create a better impression when you present some material in the form of a written loan proposal.

A thorough and well-written loan proposal can help you get your loan; a poorly prepared project can sabotage your best ideas. Think of your loan proposal as a selling tool. You're trying to sell the banker on your project so you will get the loan.

You have complete control over your loan proposal, so you can make it work. Your proposal should be logical, complete, and easy to understand. It should answer most of the questions a banker might have about your project.

Your loan proposal represents you. Although your relationship with your lending officer is important, it's unlikely that this person alone will have the authority to okay your request. The actual approval probably will be made by a senior and more experienced banker, someone you won't meet. Your written proposal will be in the office instead of you.

There's another benefit to writing a loan proposal, one that might take you by surprise: Working on the proposal can help you see your business clearly because the process of putting a plan on paper temporarily takes you out of the hectic day-to-day operations of running the company. Writing the proposal forces you, the business owner, to take an objective look at your firm. It gives you the opportunity to evaluate what you are doing so you can judge if any parts of your business are simply running on inertia.

Writing a loan proposal resulted in Connie Cross changing her perspective.

Connie's company, Northwest Interior Design, Inc., has two types of accounts: residential and commercial. Connie has divided her time and effort equally between the residential and the commercial sides of her business.

When writing her loan proposal, Connie learned a great deal about her company. After sitting down with paper and pencil, she determined that the future for her company rested with the commercial accounts and not in providing design services for residential customers. She decided that increased competition from one-person design offices had reduced her profit margins in the residential side of her business to an unacceptable level. The commercial outlook, however, was bright. New office space in her area was being developed at a rapid rate, and business owners seem to prefer working with well-established design firms like Connie's.

Based on what Connie learned while completing her loan proposal, she changed the focus of her company and substantially increased her profits.

Writing a loan proposal can help you manage your business because the cash budget and other projections provide a benchmark of what you expect to achieve in the future. You can compare the actual results with your plan.

Kit Gifford, the owner of a firm that manufactures office furniture, found the company wasn't following his plan. Sales for his firm were 18 percent below projections just four months into the year. If this trend continued, the company would not reach its goals and objectives for the year.

Kit met with key employees to discuss the causes for the discrepancy. Everyone thought that the low sales figures reflected the inadequate marketing efforts of the sales representatives. In taking corrective action, Kit decided to sponsor a sales contest.

The top sales representative for the company would win a trip to Hawaii plus a sizable bonus.

The idea worked. Sales improved dramatically over the next few months, and at year's end, profits were 6 percent above the plan's projection (a discrepancy to which Kit did not object).

I have seen all sorts of written presentations, varying from a few hand-written schedules in a manila folder to a professionally prepared proposal the size of a book. Common sense will dictate how much time and effort to put into writing a proposal. Most business owners, however, do not put enough time and effort into preparing their written proposals.

The proposal needs to be impressive in order to sell your banker—and his bosses—on the merits of your project. Plus, more than once I've seen a well-prepared proposal result in a slightly lower interest rate for the borrower.

Few proposals are as complete as the one shown in Appendix A. Just remember: When you walk into a bank for a loan, you're selling yourself, your business, and your dreams.

The Professional Loan Proposal

The initial proposal, presented at the time a banking relationship is established, is the most important one. For subsequent borrowing requests, you simply need to give your banker updated information.

The amount of effort spent in preparing a loan proposal depends on the amount you want to borrow. What's needed for a $25,000 business cycle loan is less complex than that needed for a $1,000,000 term loan. Generally, however, I recommend that all loan proposals contain the following parts:

- Cover sheet
- Cover letter
- Table of contents
- Amount and uses of loan proceeds
- History and description of the business
- Background of the management team
- Product or service market information
- Financial history

Financial projections
List of possible collateral
Personal financial statements
Exhibits

Let's review the categories one at a time.

Cover Sheet

The cover sheet is like the cover on a book. It gives the first impression to your banker, so it should be neatly typed and properly spaced on the page. Should the proposal be submitted to more than one bank, you'll need to make a separate cover sheet for each bank.

The cover sheet should identify the name of the business and the name of the person submitting the proposal. It's also a good idea to include the telephone number of the person submitting the request, so the banker can contact the appropriate person easily if there are any questions.

Cover Letter

The cover letter is an overview or summary of the financing request. It should be concise—one page—and businesslike. The letter should be addressed to a particular person so it doesn't appear to be a form letter.

The cover letter should contain:

- Your form of business (sole ownership, partnership, or corporation).
- How much money you desire.
- Why you are requesting the loan.

Table of Contents

The table of contents should follow the cover letter. Very short proposals may not need a table of contents.

Amount and Uses of Loan Proceeds

Here you state the amount of money you are requesting and how you will spend the funds. It's important to be specific, showing the banker that you have done your homework and know your financial needs.

The Wrong Way

A loan of $80,000 is being requested to pay bills and assist with the overall cash flow needs of the company.

The Right Way

A loan of $80,000 is being requested. The money will be used to pay for the company's remodeling and expansion needs. The funds will be spent as follows:

New shelving	$24,000
Additional inventory	19,000
Framing and dry wall	13,000
Flooring	8,000
Cash register	6,000
Painting	5,000
Miscellaneous	5,000
Total	$80,000

By the way, bankers don't think like car dealers; they don't bargain the amount you're going to borrow. One customer needed to borrow $35,000 but requested $40,000 because he thought the banker would counter at $30,000. The gentleman figured they would end up compromising at $35,000. Boy, was he wrong. The banker just thought the prospective borrower was poorly prepared.

History and Description of the Business

Start with the basics and write as if the reader knows nothing about you, your company, or your industry. Present the material in an informative, factual, and unemotional manner. Many entrepreneurs are enthusiastic. They're excited about their companies, so it is easy for them to use emotional words like *fantastic, tremendous,* and *phenomenal.* Remember that although the written proposal is a sales tool, it is going to be read by bankers. You are not writing the keynote speech at an Amway convention. From a banker's perspective, hype and rah-rah are used by snake oil salesmen.

So try to restrain yourself and let the facts speak for themselves. Be sure to include:

- The nature of the business.
- How long the business has been in existence.
- Location of the company.
- Whether it is a sole ownership, partnership, or corporation.
- Significant changes that have occurred during the past few years.
- Future plans.

The Wrong Way

For many years, Salem Office Supply has enjoyed an excellent reputation. We have this reputation because of our commitment to excellence and meeting the needs of our customers. Our sales force is hardworking and dedicated to providing quality customer service. Combining this with the loyalty and support of our operational staff, we are confident that this coming year will be profitable and rewarding.

The Right Way

Salem Office Supply, a sole proprietorship, is owned by Oliver Brinkerhoff. The company was established in 19X3 and for the past 12 years has been a wholesaler of office supplies.

The firm has grown and prospered over the years. Starting with only Oliver and his wife as employees, the firm now has a staff of 11 and sales of over $1,500,000.

Last year the company moved into its new warehouse and offices located at 2214 Yale Avenue East in Salem. Within a few years, the owner would like to open a second distribution outlet in the town of Eugene.

If you are establishing a new business, make this section even more comprehensive. An established company has a track record that the banker can review. A start-up company has only the dreams and plans of its owner.

Thus, in a pragmatic and logical manner, you need to convince your banker that you know what you are doing. Whenever possible, support your position with facts and figures. Answer these questions in your proposal:

- Since most new business ventures fail, why is your firm going to be successful?
- What specific marketing plans does your company have to help it obtain a share of the marketplace?
- How will your company differ from its competition?

For business owners taking over an existing business, a few other questions need to be addressed:

- How long has the business been in existence?
- Who are the current owners?
- How long have the current owners been running the business?
- Why is the business for sale?
- Why will your managerial ability help the company?
- How was the acquisition price arrived at? (Here the banker is interested in your thought processes: Did you do your homework and negotiate a good deal? Or were you swept away by enthusiasm? I remember one new entrepreneur who told me he arrived at the price because "that's what the owner was asking.")

Background of the Management Team

It's not the products or services that make any business a success; it's the people in the organization. This is true at all levels, but the most important employees are the ones at the top who make the key decisions.

A banker wants to know a lot about top managers: What is their experience? How many years have they been in the business? (If appropriate, mention their educational background.) Is their competency in all the managerial functions (operations, marketing, finance, and personnel)? If not, what actions are being taken to eliminate the deficiencies?

What plans have been decided for management succession? Many companies are operated by one person. If a truck runs over the owner, what would happen to the company? Remember, a banker wants to know that the loan will be repaid—even if the business owner isn't around to do it. By mentioning these points, even briefly, in a loan proposal, you can make a favorable impression on your banker.

The Wrong Way

Oliver Brinkerhoff handles the sales and operations of the firm. He is supported by his wife, who works two days a week, and a bookkeeper, Jerri Mitchell. The company also employs three salesmen: Richard Long, Carl Schuster, and Red Thompson.

The company has two sales clerks, two truck drivers, and three stock boys.

The Right Way

Oliver Brinkerhoff, 46, has worked in the wholesale office supply business for over 23 years. He spent three years as assistant manager for Jake's Paper and Pencils. During the next 11 years, he worked for the national chain of Kelly Office Products, starting as store manager and moving up to district manager. During his last two years at Kelly, he was regional manager with the responsibility of supervising 14 different retail stores. He left Kelly to establish Salem Office Supply.

Most of the managerial decisions are made jointly by Oliver and his wife, JoAnn. While JoAnn works only part time, she has been actively involved in the management of the company since its inception.

Richard Long, senior sales representative, has been with the company for eight years. Richard has good insight into the marketplace and is involved with key marketing decisions.

Lynne Morrell, senior sales clerk, is very knowledgeable and has been with the firm for two years. She is responsible for the service function when Oliver and JoAnn are away from the office.

Product or Service Market Information

What are the primary products or services offered? What about the product mix? Does the company specialize in one product or two, or does it offer a wide spectrum of products to the marketplace? Has there been a trend or direction change in recent years?

Who are the customers and the competitors? What is the company's niche in the marketplace? Equally important is what the business owner is doing to maintain or improve market share. Covering these points shows bankers that the owners are looking toward the future rather that just struggling to get by.

Whenever possible, it's best to be specific and use facts, figures, and names rather than state broad generalities. The library, local chamber of commerce, and trade associations are excellent resources for statistical information. So is the Small Business Administration. Too often the comments in this section of the proposal are enthusiastic but unsupportable generalizations.

The Wrong Way

Salem Office Supply serves a number of accounts in the greater Salem area. Many of its clients have been with the firm for a number of years and are very loyal.

Although the company has a solid account base, the sales representatives are ambitious in soliciting new accounts.

The Right Way

The company provides a broad range of office supplies—everything from pencils and erasers to portable typewriters.

At this time, approximately 380 accounts are served, most of them in the greater Salem area. The distribution of sales to total revenues is as follows:

Large commercial accounts	45%
Retail office supply stores	34%
Supermarkets/grocery stores	14%
Retail computer stores	7%

Historically the large commercial accounts have been the main source of revenues for the firm. First National Bank,

Ballard Insurance, and the City of Salem have been the three largest purchasers of office supplies. This market is competitive; nevertheless, most of the major accounts appear to be content with the products, prices, and service offered by the company.

Recently the company has been very successful in selling computer paper, printer ribbons, and related products to retail computer stores. The main reason the company is able to penetrate this market is that Salem Office Supply offers computer paper at prices below those of the competition. This is possible because last year Salem signed an exclusive agreement with RJB Paper Products in Canada. The agreement allows Salem Office Supply to acquire large quantities of computer paper at a favorable price.

In the coming year, sales to retail computer stores are expected to represent 11 percent of total sales.

Financial History

To make a good impression, financial statements need to be complete and accurate. (Of course, recently established businesses can't provide historical information.)

Bankers like to look at trends. If possible, it's best to include the last three fiscal year-end statements (balance sheets and income statements). Make sure that the net worth reconciles from one year to the next. If it's been a number of months since the annual statements were prepared, an interim balance sheet and income statement should be submitted. The most recent statement should not be over 90 days old.

It's also best to include tax returns. For corporations, this would be corporate returns; otherwise, include personal tax returns. Like annual financial statements, the tax returns should cover the past three years.

Some firms have a great deal of accounts receivable and accounts payable. In such cases, most bankers prefer to have a listing, called an *aging*. It indicates the names, the amounts due, and whether the particular account is current or past due. Those that are past due are usually grouped into 30-day increments.

Financial Projections

It's advisable to submit a pro forma income statement, cash budget, and pro forma balance sheet, prepared for the coming fiscal year.

If you are projecting the cash budget beyond one year, quarterly estimates are usually adequate. The projections need to be realistic. Overly optimistic projections can create an unfavorable impression with your banker and hurt your credibility.

All three projections are beneficial. Depending on the situation, you may want to footnote basic assumptions used in preparing the projections—for example, "Sales are expected to increase by 14 percent in the coming year. This compares to a sales growth of 13 percent last year and an increase of 14 percent in the previous year."

List of Possible Collateral

This section may not be necessary, but when you include it, you demonstrate some financial sophistication and knowledge.

Sometimes the true or market value is different from that listed on the balance sheet. For instance, real estate could be on the sheet at its purchase price; however, the property might be worth a great deal more because of appreciation. When listing possible collateral, it's best to show both the cost and the fair market value. To give a complete picture, also list any liens against the possible collateral.

Personal Financial Statements

Unless a company is very solid financially, it's common for a banker to ask the business owner to guarantee or stand behind the bank loan personally. Since the financial strength of the owner is a factor in approving the loan, a copy of the owner's personal financial statement needs to be included. The personal statement needs to have been prepared within the past six months.

Exhibits

Any other pertinent information that might be of interest to the bankers needs to be in this section. Such items might include:

- Plans or blueprints.
- Pictures.
- Legal documents.
- Quotations or estimates.
- Census or demographic data.

In short, preparing a written loan proposal takes time, but it's well worth the effort. Bankers must have this information so they can evaluate your financing request.

Once you put together a well-prepared loan proposal, you're ready to set up an appointment with a bank officer. How this meeting goes can mean the difference between success (your getting your loan) and failure (no cash). Chapter 11 tells you what you need to know to have a profitable meeting.

CHAPTER 11

Presenting Your Loan Request

Bankers and entrepreneurs have some interesting discussions about borrowing needs over a conference table. Once Dick Hunt, an experienced banker, met with a man who wanted to borrow $38,000 for seed money to start a car wash. After about 30 minutes of discussion, Dick asked the man if he had brought a written loan proposal or financial statements.

The customer indicated that he had but that he had accidently left it in the car. He went out to the car, got in, and drove off. That was the last Dick ever saw of the customer or heard about the car wash. The poor guy was probably as nervous as a turkey during the latter part of November.

Fred Nelson, another banker, has a different kind of story. One afternoon a dapperly dressed man waked into Fred's office and after some initial chitchat asked, "How long will it take to get a $100,000 loan approved?"

Fred responded, "It shouldn't take too long. Probably three or four days."

"I bet you can do it faster than that," said the would-be borrower as he pulled a handgun from underneath his coat. "Let's go to the vault."

When telling the story, Fred says he learned the true meaning of the old expression, "The customer is always right."

If you're one of those people who feel anxious and self-conscious walking into a bank and requesting a loan, I understand how you feel. But look at the bright side: You're not going to the dentist to have a molar extracted or in for an audit by the IRS. You are simply offering the banker the opportunity to assist you with your need, and the bank makes a quality loan that will be repaid with interest. Always remember: Bankers need borrowers just as much as borrowers need bankers.

When approaching a banker for a loan, follow this important rule: Always present your loan request far in advance of when you actually need the cash. I say this for two reasons:

1. It takes time to get loans approved.
2. Bankers do not like being pushed. It makes them anxious, and a nervous banker is much less likely to approve your loan.

Let's look at each of these points.

It does take time to get loans approved, especially when you are establishing a new banking relationship or requesting a sizable increase in the amount of money being borrowed. For reasons that I'll explain in a later chapter, most of the time, it will take at least a couple of days for a banker to approve a request. Frequently the time frame needed for a decision is a couple of weeks or longer. Most banks are bureaucratic organizations with lots of red tape and paperwork.

My second point is that bankers don't like to be pushed. When a business owner says, "I need the money as soon as possible," a red flag goes up in the banker's mind. The lending officer wonders: If the customer is that desperate for a loan, can he really be creditworthy? Besides, a rushed customer appears to be someone who doesn't have a good backup plan. The banker's assumptions may be wrong; what matters is that these perceptions can hurt or help you.

Always call ahead and make an appointment with your banker. Like attorneys and accountants, bankers are professionals. It's important that they have a sufficient amount of time to discuss your financial needs fully. Unfortunately, too many customers just drop by and hope to get a few minutes of their time. This is also a mistake.

One day a middle-aged man stopped by my office and asked if we could chat for a couple of minutes. I didn't have an appointment and was able to meet with him. He then presented a loan request for $6.5 million! The request made sense, and the loan was eventually made; however, with his successful background and the amount of money he needed, I was amazed that he didn't call ahead for an appointment.

When deciding whether to approve a loan request, a banker considers the applicant's financial records, payment habits, and abilities. Your loan request presentation needs to be well prepared and organized, and so do you. In a sense, the situation is just like a professional salesperson making a sales presentation. You are selling yourself.

Some business people have what they call their "banker's uniform": a dark suit, a white shirt, and a maroon tie or scarf. Before visiting the bank, one successful rock musician used to remove his single diamond earring. For him, that was his "banker's uniform." (In his case, it didn't matter what he wore because he made almost $1 million each year. Bankers loved lending him money.)

Where you live and what you do affects what you should wear when visiting your banker. How you dress as an executive working in downtown Manhattan is much different from how you dress if you are a wheat farmer in Kennewick, Washington. It's a fact of life that people make judgments about us based on our appearance. Remember that your number one goal is to make a favorable impression on the banker and his or her superiors. A neat and tidy appearance does make a difference.

I know many bankers who say the most difficult part of their job is discussing loan requests with new borrowers. Interviewing is not easy, especially when the person sitting on the other side of the desk wants some money. And let's face it, the interviewing skills of bankers vary. Some loan officers are relaxed, others intense. Most are organized (an important skill for a banker), but some are not. Some have excellent human relations skills; others do not.

Since there are no guarantees that your banker will be an effective interviewer and listener, you can help yourself by being very well prepared.

If the banker doesn't raise an important point and the answer is in your favor, raise it yourself, and supply the response.

On the other hand, there are basic questions a banker will always ask. Knowing what to expect is half the battle.

Questions Bankers Will Always Ask

When I was a banker, I always asked a business borrower five basic questions:

1. Can you give me some background information about yourself and your firm?
2. How much money do you want to borrow?
3. What are you going to do with the money?
4. How do you plan to repay the bank?
5. Did you bring some financial information?

By using these five relatively nonthreatening questions, usually the conversation flowed reasonably well. Equally important, I obtained the information I needed. This format helped me so I didn't need to bother the customer again with a long list of questions.

All bankers have their own style, but there is a benefit to following this sequential order. I would frequently overhear one associate or another start a conversation by asking the amount of money desired. Then a discussion about financial reports would follow, and next he would talk about possible collateral. This is unfortunate, because the banker would not fully understand the borrower's background and needs.

You as a business owner must sell yourself, your skills, and your ideas. Therefore, if a banker starts the conversation by saying, "So, you would like to borrow some money. How much would you like to borrow?" I suggest your response should be, "Yes, I would like to borrow some money. But before we talk about that, let me briefly give you some background information about me and my firm."

If the banker isn't exactly sure of your situation or doesn't understand your reply to one of his questions, he will ask additional questions. Let's examine some common follow-up questions in the five basic areas that I've outlined.

First question: "Can you give me some background information about yourself and your firm?"

Possible Follow-Up Questions

- What is your background and experience in your line of work?
- Are there other owners? If so, who are they, what is their background, and what share of the company do they own?
- How long has the business been in existence?
- Is the firm a sole proprietorship, partnership, or corporation?
- Is this a manufacturing, wholesale, retail, or service company?
- What products and/or services do you offer?
- Who are your major customers?
- Who are your competitors?
- What types of financing terms does your company usually offer?
- What geographical area do you serve?
- Who are the key members of the management team, and what is their background?
- Is there a plan for management succession?
- What kinds of insurance coverage do you maintain?
- What are your plans for the future?

Second and third questions: "How much money do you want to borrow?" "What are you going to use the money for?"

Possible Follow-Up Questions

- How much money do you need?
- How are you going to spend the money?
- Do you have a list of how you intend to use the money?

Fourth question: "How do you plan to repay the bank?"

Possible Follow-Up Questions

- If your plans don't materialize as expected, then how are you going to pay back the bank?

- Do you plan on repaying the debt by conversion of assets into cash or by profits?
- If necessary, do you have additional money that you could put into the firm?

Fifth question: "Did you bring some financial information?"

Possible Follow-Up Questions

- When is the fiscal year-end for your company?
- Do you prepare interim statements?
- Where do you maintain your bank accounts?
- Do you use more than one bank?
- Did you happen to bring an aging of your accounts receivable? (Remember, this is a list of accounts that owe you money.)
- Are any accounts severely past due or unlikely to be collected?
- What is your normal charge-off experience?
- How is your inventory valued?
- Who are your major suppliers?
- Do you normally take trade discounts?
- Did you bring an aging of accounts payable?
- Do you have any contingent liabilities?
- What has been the sales trend?
- What has been the profit picture in recent years?
- Do you have a current personal financial statement?
- Did you bring financial projections?
- Do you have any other information I should review?

Depending on what is said, bankers might ask additional questions. Also, they probably will have some more questions after reviewing the financial reports.

Interview Guidelines

Following a few simple guidelines during an interview can greatly improve your chances of having your loan approved.

1. *Tell both the good and the bad.* One of my bosses used to say, "Would-be borrowers are always optimists." When making a loan request, it is easy to overemphasize all the positive aspects of a business venture and omit everything else. Remember, though, that the best relationship is built on credibility. Be sure you present all the pertinent facts.

Fairway Auto Body, an automobile body repair shop, has several major accounts. Most of the company's revenues come from insurance companies. Since insurance companies often are slow in processing the necessary paperwork, Fairway uses a credit line. Money provided under the line covers the company's expenses until it receives payments from the insurance companies.

Jack, the owner, asked me to increase his credit line from $150,000 to $200,000. He said the increase in the line was needed since his business was booming and he had just signed an agreement with the local BMW dealer to do all of its auto body work. He estimated the new BMW agreement was going to boost Fairway's annual revenues by about 15 percent. That was the good news.

Later, I found out out there was another piece to the puzzle. True, Jack had signed a contract with the BMW dealer; however, I also learned he was in the middle of a dispute with an insurance company. Apparently the insurance company supervisor was dissatisfied with the quality of Fairway's work. He was refusing to pay several large invoices. This dispute was the cause of Jack's dried-up cash flow and the reason he needed to borrow more money from the bank.

Needless to say, Jack's unwillingness to tell the entire story did not inspire confidence in me. In fact, his behavior caused me to keep a sharp eye on his accounts.

2. *If you don't understand what your banker is saying, ask questions.* Most people have a tendency to talk the jargon of their industry. Bankers are no exception. If a banker starts using words or terms you don't understand, ask for clarification.

Amos Anderson, an attorney, once approached me to borrow a sizable amount of money to buy an office building as an investment. He wanted to buy the building and pay for it over a number of years.

In discussing his financial statements, I made the comment that his practice had a negative working capital position. (Current assets were less than current liabilities.) Because of this, I was concerned about his being able to make the monthly payments to the bank. I felt perhaps his cash flow would be too tight.

After Amos completed a cash budget, I no longer had a concern, and the loan was made. Later, however, I learned that he thought *working capital* was just another word for *net worth.* Amos couldn't understand why I had said he had a negative working capital (net worth) when he had over $300,000 invested in his practice.

Obviously, I made a mistake by using financial jargon and not fully explaining my concerns. However, it would have been to Amos Anderson's advantage to ask for clarification.

3. *Always mention a secondary repayment source.* Bankers are trained to focus on how the bank will be repaid if the primary means of repayment goes sour. Beat your banker to the punch: When making a loan request, always mention a primary and alternative means of repayment, thus demonstrating that you have done your homework.

Stan Coyle, owner of Springfield Garage Doors, needed a new flatbed truck to use in his business of installing and servicing commercial and industrial garage doors.

"I'd like to borrow $37,000 for the purchase of a new truck," said Stan to his banker. "This cash budget shows I'll have plenty of money to pay back the bank.

"Of course, I'm willing to pledge the truck as collateral," he added. "That way, if something unforeseen happens, you'll have a solid secondary means of repayment."

4. *Fill out all forms completely, accurately, and to the best of your ability.* Frequently applicants complete only a portion of the credit application or other forms because they feel adequate information already has been provided elsewhere. This may be true, but bankers frequently see this lack of thoroughness as an indication of the way the customer handles other financial affairs. Rather than take the chance of creating a negative impression, complete the document.

5. *Never bluff. If you don't know an answer to a question, admit it.* The banker asked Arnie Olson why the prepaid expenses on his balance sheet were so much higher than they were last year.

"I don't know," Arnie responded to his banker. "Let me do some research, and I'll get back to you with the answer tomorrow."

Since he didn't have the answer, Arnie had handled the situation properly. His response was direct and honest.

Don't fudge; it's always much better to admit you don't know. You can say you will find out and telephone with the information. Guessing is risky; if you are wrong, a banker may question your credibility on other points.

By knowing your financing needs and following these guidelines, information should flow smoothly between you and your banker.

One more bit of advice: Try not to take the whole process too seriously. You aren't the first person who has felt uncomfortable at a banker's desk. Unless you are a frequent borrower, it's not easy to go a bank, expose your financial health, and let another person pass judgment on whether you are going to be lent some money.

You're probably curious about the fate of your proposal once you leave the bank. I explain what happens to it in the next chapter.

CHAPTER 12

What Happens After You Leave the Bank

After you leave the bank, your efforts to get the loan can stop—temporarily. Your banker's work has just begun:

1. Read the written loan proposal
2. Analyze the financial reports and projections
3. Check the payment history for you, the business owner, and for your company

After reviewing all this information, a loan officer usually has a fairly definite opinion about whether the bank should lend you the money. In the worst-case scenario, the banker will contact you and explain why he must turn down your loan application. (And if he doesn't explain fully, ask questions.) In happier circumstances, however, the banker believes you are a good credit risk and must proceed as follows:

- Decide what collateral, if any, will be required.
- Decide the repayment schedule.
- Determine the interest rate for the loan.
- Determine whether to give you a loan or establish a credit line.
- Obtain formal approval, if necessary, from a senior banker.
- Prepare the necessary documents for you to sign.
- Give you the money and complete the paperwork.

Let's focus on checking the payment history of you and your company and on how to obtain formal approval from a senior banker. (The remaining points are discussed in other chapters.)

Your Payment Record

Bankers want to know if business owners pay their bills on time. Experience has taught them that people are creatures of habit. If a businessman has traditionally paid his obligations on time, that trend will probably continue. If that has not been the case, then . . . [you can complete the rest of the sentence].

The vast majority of the time, a banker will ask a business owner to stand behind or personally guarantee the loans for his company, so it makes sense for the banker to check the payment history of the business owner and the company. Thus, the process of checking the payment history for each is slightly different.

Individual Credit Reports

Checking the payment habits of individuals has become a automated process. Credit-granting companies—like department stores, utility companies, and banks—send payment activity information to a centralized agency, called a credit reporting bureau. The agency compiles the data and provides information to companies that request it. (The receiving companies pay the agency a fee for the information.)

The information supplied on the report can be divided into several categories.

First, the report gives statistical information about the applicant, such as name, home address, and occupation. Next listed is a summation of public records, like judgments and data from collection agencies.

Bankers want to stay away from any customers with problems. If there is a single report of a bill being turned over for collection, the loan officer probably will dismiss this claim as a dispute; however, a list of many accounts turned over to collection agencies is certainly the kiss of death for someone who wants a loan approved.

The next section reports previous inquiries made by credit-granting companies. You might think this section is not very important, but in fact most bankers are especially cautious of entrepreneurs who apply for loans at several financial institutions. I recall a businessman who came into my bank and said, "My wife wanted me to go to another bank for a loan. However, I decided to come to you first since you guys have the best reputation in town."

We had a good interview, and after he left, I ordered a credit report. What do you think I found? That this customer had been applying to many banks in town. I made a few phone calls and discovered that he had told many of my fellow bankers they had "the best reputation in town." Needless to say, this businessman's credibility took a nosedive.

The final section contains a credit history: the name (or identification number) of the creditor, when the account was opened, and the account number. The report also includes the credit limit, high balance, current balance, number of times delinquent, and severity of the delinquencies. The credit history is the most valuable section of the report. From a banker's perspective, a good payment record is vital.

If you want to review a copy of your credit report, you can. This information is available to you by federal law. To find the bureau in your area, look in the telephone directory under "Credit Reporting Agencies" or "Credit Bureaus" (or ask your local banker). You need to present proper identification to obtain this information. If you want a copy of your report, there is a nominal fee.

Company Payment Records

The credit report shows whether business owners pay their bills on time. Bankers also want to know how promptly a firm pays its trade suppliers. This information is obtained from mercantile agencies and credit bureaus such as the National Association of Credit Management and Dun & Bradstreet. The report shows the highest amount of credit extended to the firm, amounts outstanding, and the terms of sale. What's relevant is how promptly the company pays its suppliers and the length of time it has used suppliers. The shorter the credit history, the less a banker can rely on the information. Some reports also include information about when a company began business, background information on the principals, and a brief financial history.

A banker may compare the amount of money a company owes, according to the mercantile reports, with what is listed on the company's balance sheet. This comparison is especially likely for small companies where the owner prepares the financial information. Occasionally the amount listed on the mercantile report differs significantly from the amount shown on the balance sheet. In such a case, a banker investigates to learn the reasons for the discrepancy.

Loan-Approval Process

Having good judgment about loans is a major requirement of a successful banker. Typically newcomers to banking start out as junior lending officers and climb the corporate ladder to assistant vice president and then vice president. Those who are gifted (or lucky) may even reach senior vice president or president. As bankers go up in title and salary, they look at larger and more complex requests for money.

Every loan officer has a lending limit. It could be as low as $5,000 or run into the millions. A banker can approve or decline all loan requests at or below the lending limit. A banker also has the authority to decline requests above the assigned limit. An officer who thinks the bank should grant a loan above the specified limit needs to obtain the approval of a higher level of authority.

Here's an example of the loan officer's lending limit for the Second National Bank:

Board of Directors	After-the-fact review
Senior Loan Committee	All over $3,000,000
Phil Roppo, President	$3,000,000

Terri Fridgen, Executive Vice President	$2,000,000
Mike McPherson, Senior Vice President	$1,000,000
Joe Berruezo, Vice President	$500,000
Scott Dills, Vice President	$200,000
Robert Plough, Assistant Vice President	$75,000
Vikki Walters, Manager	$50,000
Dawn Bjorn, Assistant Manager	$25,000
Luther Toothman, Lending Officer	$10,000

Here's how the system works. Dr. Paul Painfree, a dentist, presents Ms. Walters with a $45,000 loan request. He wants to buy a new piece of dental equipment. Since the amount is within her level of authority, Ms. Walters can approve or decline the dentist's loan application. But if Dr. Painfree decides he needs $175,000 to undertake a major renovation of his office and equipment, Ms. Walters will have to get approval from her superiors.

With the larger request, Ms. Walters's first move is to present the loan application to Mr. Plough for his approval.

Let's say Mr. Plough does not think the bank can lend Dr. Painfree $175,000 because the dentist doesn't have enough money coming in from his patients to make the payments on a loan of that size. In that case, Ms. Walters will contact Dr. Painfree and explain why the bank won't be able to participate in his project.

Let's suppose, however, that Dr. Painfree has a spotless credit record, plenty of assets, and an adequate cash flow to make the monthly payments. Mr. Plough is delighted to lend him $175,000 at the prevailing rate of interest, but he can't okay the loan. He must go upstairs to Mr. Dills, whose lending limit is $200,000. If Mr. Plough approves, Dr. Painfree gets his money—and the request has the blessings of three bankers: Ms. Walters, Mr. Plough, and Mr. Dills.

The Loan Committee

When talking to customers, a banker may say that the loan request needs to go "to the loan committee." Depending on the bank, this powerful committee may have three, four, or more bankers. Much of the time, however, a loan application never has to go to a committee; it is reviewed by a bank officer with higher lending limits.

It's crucial to realize that when you apply for a loan, you seldom have the opportunity to present your request to the bank officer who actually can approve it—or to the loan committee. (The more money you want, the more this is true, as Dr. Painfree discovered.) Most banks have deliberately established a barrier between the borrowers and the approving personnel.

Loan-approval bankers are busy. They spend their day approving and declining requests for a number of subordinates. Besides, in the banking world, it is thought that personal contact with the applicant can sometimes influence a banker to make a poor decision. It is felt a higher-level bank officer can be more objective. This person will make a decision based on the facts rather than being emotionally involved in the decision. Being a step removed from the process is part of the system of checks and balances in banking. For these reasons, you usually will not know the identity of the person or persons approving your loan request.

Where does that leave you? It means your loan proposal is all the more important. However competent your banker, it's likely that a senior officer—a complete stranger to you—will approve your loan. Almost always, this high-level banker will review your written proposal. As a former senior loan officer, I can't stress enough how much the proposal represents you. An impressive and detailed proposal can be your best tool to sell the banker on the merits of your project.

What to Do If Your Loan Proposal Is Rejected

If your banker—or someone with a higher level of lending authority—approves your loan, you'll receive the money you need. Unfortunately, in the real world, not all loan requests are approved. Should your banker decline your financing request, ask some probing questions. You'll learn a lot from the answers.

When declining a loan request, some bankers give a wishy-washy answer like "the loan committee turned it down" or "your request doesn't meet our guidelines." If this is the "reason" given, push for definite explanations. Your questions probably won't change the banker's mind, but you deserve to know exactly why the bank does not think your request is acceptable. That way you can overcome the potential concerns when making your next presentation.

It's important to remember that decisions about lending money are subjective. I know of one woman who made basically the same presentation to eleven different bankers before she got financing. The first ten chose not to participate in her project; the eleventh banker was truly excited about it.

Assuming your loan request is approved, the next step is for you to discuss the interest rate on your loan. That's the topic of the next chapter.

CHAPTER 13

Negotiate Interest Rates!

If your company is financially successful, the most important point to remember about interest rates is that they are negotiable.

Depending on the amount of money borrowed, negotiating a slightly lower rate can save thousands of dollars. Gail Crowley, the owner of Management Consultants, Inc., approached her banker and asked for a $200,000 credit line to help pay expenses until money is collected from her customers. After reviewing the company's financial statements, the banker agreed to set up the credit line and quoted Gail an interest rate of 11.5 percent. While Gail was appreciative of the banker's approving her request, she felt 11.5 percent was too high.

"I don't think I should have to pay more than 11 percent," said Gail. "If you can set up the line at that rate, then I'm interested. Otherwise maybe I'll pursue some other options."

"Let me see what I can do," responded the banker. "I'll give you a call tomorrow."

The following day, the banker called Gail and said, "I just talked to my boss, and we can give you the 11 percent. We normally don't do this type of thing, but you are a valuable customer of this bank. I can have the paperwork ready next Tuesday. Is that okay?"

Management Consultants is a financially strong and well-managed company. By assertively asking for a lower interest rate, the owner is saving the company thousands of dollars.

Al Eikins's story is even more impressive. Al is a certified public accountant and needs $625,000 to build a new office building. Al's negotiations with his banker resulted in his loan rate being reduced from 10.5 percent to 10 percent. Al figures the lower rate on his mortgage will save him almost $35,000 over the next 15 years.

Factors Determining Interest Rate

To be a good negotiator, you need to understand the seven factors a banker considers in determining the interest rate to change a customer. They are:

1. The bank's cost of funds.
2. The perceived risk to the bank.
3. The repayment period of the loan.
4. The amount of money being borrowed.
5. The bank's handling costs (the time and effort it takes a banker to process a loan).
6. The average balance on deposit.
7. The competition.

Let's review these items one at a time.

Bank's Cost of Funds

The difference between the interest a bank pays its depositors and the interest it collects from borrowers has to cover the bank's expenses. The funds left over come under that most favorite of categories, profits. The most important factor that determines the rate of interest charged to a business owner is the bank's *cost of funds.* In lay terms, this means what the bank has to pay to obtain its supply of money.

You can see the basic relationship between the rate banks pay on savings instruments and the rate it charges borrowers. When the rates paid on savings instruments are low, borrowing rates also will be relatively low. When the rates paid to savers are high, banks will pass this increased cost on to their borrowers.

Perceived Risk to the Bank

Here the rule is simple: The higher is the perceived risk by the bank, the higher is the rate.

Once a banker decides to give you a loan, you're considered creditworthy. But there is creditworthy and CREDITWORTHY—a difference in *how* creditworthy affects the interest rate you pay.

Banks offer their lowest interest rate to their best customers. While no loan is ever completely risk free, a loan to a new mom-and-pop hamburger stand has more risk than a loan to McDonalds or Burger King, well-established, financially solid companies.

Repayment Period of the Loan

The longer the time needed to repay the loan, the higher the interest rate.

The further we look into the future, the more uncertainty we see. From a banker's viewpoint, uncertainty is just another word for *risk,* a word the average loan officer regards with much distaste. Since the interest rate charged is a reflection of risk, loans repaid over several years are charged a higher rate than loans that will be repaid in the near future.

Amount of Money Being Borrowed

Usually borrowing a large rather than a small amount of money results in your being charged a lower interest rate. It's cheaper for a banker to administer one loan of $500,000 than to handle 20 loans of $25,000. Because the administrative cost per dollar loaned is less, the rate charged customers is lower.

Bank's Handling Costs

The more paperwork and review the bank needs to do for a loan, the higher the interest rate is. Imagine that you and a colleague each borrow the same amount of money from the bank. You qualify for an unsecured loan; the banker requires your friend to pledge collateral for his loan. Your friend is going to be charged a higher interest rate. His loan will cost him more because it costs the bank more.

Some collateralized loans, such as those secured by accounts receivable or inventory, require continual monitoring by bank personnel. This is one of the reasons why the rate charged customers is so high when these assets are pledged as collateral.

Average Balance on Deposit

Many customers often think in terms of the dollars that flow through their accounts. But bankers have a different perspective: They care about how much *stays* in the bank. If you deposit $100,000 in the morning and withdraw the same amount in the afternoon, the banker sees some paperwork and not much else.

The average amount of money you leave in your account is important to the banker: The higher the average, the better. The more money there is in the bank, the more loans the banker can make. And the more loans the bank makes, the more profit it realizes.

As part of the loan-negotiating process, some banks require borrowers to maintain a certain amount of money in their checking accounts. For instance, you may request to borrow $250,000. As part of the negotiating process, the banker asks you to maintain an average balance in your checking account of $25,000 or more. The common term used for this type of arrangement is *compensating balance.*

Competition

In the not-so-distant past, competition in the banking industry was practically nonexistent. Bankers simply served their own customers and seldom solicited the accounts of other banks.

Fortunately, those times have changed. In 1980, Congress passed the Depository Institutions Deregulation and Monetary Control Act, perhaps the most significant banking legislation since the Federal Reserve Act of 1913. This act mandated the orderly deregulation of the banking industry.

As you can imagine, the deregulation process has been very painful for many bankers. Conservative bankers who are quick to state policies and guidelines are losing customers; those who provide high-quality service at competitive prices are gaining new accounts. Most of the time, loan officers would rather offer a good customer a lower rate of interest than have the person move to the competition. Bankers have been forced to improve the quality of their service and trim their profit margins. The days of the "3-6-3" rule—pay depositors 3 percent, loan the same money out at 6 percent, and be on the golf course by 3 P.M. are past.

The Bottom Line

Together, the seven factors just discussed determine the interest rate a customer will be charged. No one single factor is crucial; however, you can help yourself negotiate your interest rate if you remember two simple rules:

1. The higher the risk to the bank, the higher the interest rate.
2. The more you borrow, the more flexibility the banker has in negotiating.

When negotiating a lower interest rate, always put yourself in the shoes of the banker. Try to think of a way that will reduce the risk of your loan to the bank. For instance, the interest rate on unsecured loans is usually lower than with collateralized loans. If, however, you are willing to pledge General Motors common stock as collateral, then the banker may charge you a lower rate of interest than if the loan is unsecured. The reason is that the risk to the bank is less. If you are unable to make your payments, the banker will sell the stock and pay off the loan. The lower risk results in a lower interest rate being charged.

Let's take another example. Short-term loans normally have a lower interest rate than long-term loans. If a short-term loan is unsecured and a bank savings certificate secures a long-term loan, the latter loan would have a lower interest rate because of the reduced risk to the bank.

Figure 13-1 provides some guidance for your negotiations on interest rates.

- Get your loan approved first. Don't try to negotiate price before you know you're getting the money.
- Ask under what conditions the rate would be less.
- Consider shortening the term of the loan or using different collateral (e.g., common stock instead of equipment) to lower the rate.
- Emphasize the fact that you are a loyal customer. Bankers still like that. (Remember, when you apply for a loan, the banker will get a credit report that shows credit inquiries from other banks, so he will know if you shop around all the time.)

Figure 13-1. Four steps for negotiating with your banker.

The Prime Rate

Most banks call their lowest rate their *prime rate.* This term originated in the 1930s. Over the years, the prime rate has undergone considerable fluctuation. In the 1930s, it was as low as 1.5 percent. In 1980, it skyrocketed to a high of 21.5 percent.

To assist lending officers in deciding which rate to offer a customer, a bank's top management issues interest rate guidelines.

When presented with a proposal, a banker refers to the guidelines in Figure 13-2 and selects an appropriate rate. For example, a lending officer has decided to lend a borrower $155,000 for 90 days without requiring collateral. The banker would refer to the unsecured category for loans between $100,001 and $250,000. He would see that the suggested rate for this type of loan is between 15.25 and 15.75 percent (the base rate of 15.50 percent, plus or minus 0.25 percent).

Up-Front Fees

Many banks are now charging up-front fees in addition to the annual interest rate. These fees are commonly called *points,* with 1 point being equal to 1 percent of the loan amount. If the business owner is charged 1 point on a $200,000 loan, the

Figure 13-2. Business loan interest rate guidelines.

Second National Bank
Prime rate, 4-12-X2, 13.75%

Base Rate	Amount
17.50%	Up to $25,000
16.50%	$25,001–50,000
16.00%	$50,001–100,000
15.50%	$100,001–250,000
15.00%	$250,001–500,000
14.50%	$500,001–1,000,000
14.00%	Over $1,000,000

Loan Type	Suggested Rate
Unsecured	Base rate + or − .25%
Assigned accounts receivable	Base rate + .75% to 1.25%
Equipment, fixtures	Base rate + .75% to 1.25%
Crop, livestock, farm products	Base rate + .50% to 1.00%
Inventory, warehouse receipts	Base rate + 1.00% to 1.50%
Marketable stocks and bonds	Base rate − .25% to + .75%
Savings, bonds, certificates of deposit	Base rate − .75% to + 1.25%
Term loans	Base rate + 1.75% to 2.25%

Loan Maturity	Suggested Loan Fee
Less than 1 year	.5 to 1.0
1 to 3 years	1.0 to 1.5
Over 3 years	1.5 to 2.0

up-front fee is $2,000. Points are a method whereby banks can increase their income since the fee is paid at the time the loan is made. It's a particularly common system.

Sometimes a banker will offer some options. One might be to make the loan at the bank's prime interest rate plus 1.5 percent with 2 points. Another would be to have the loan at the bank's prime rate plus 2 percent with 1 point. You get to choose the option. Both alternatives result in about the same return for the bank. The lower annual interest rate is simply offset by a higher up-front fee.

Most borrowers accept the up-front points offered by a banker. But this may not be a wise decision. Owners of well-established, highly profitable, and financially strong companies should probably ask for lower points. Often a banker will reduce either the interest rate or lower the fees so the customer doesn't go to another bank.

Spend a couple of minutes negotiating. You could save yourself a considerable amount of money. In fact, as a banker, I respected entrepreneurs who let me know the interest rate or points I offered were too high. I usually found these people to be good businessmen and businesswomen.

If you have to borrow a considerable amount of money, consider comparing rates with another bank. Today's bankers are much more aggressive in obtaining new business than they were a few years ago. One of my favorite customers said, "The color of the money is all the same. It just comes down to the quality of service provided and how much the bank wants to charge for the use of its money."

CHAPTER 14

The Paper Trail

Movie mogul Samuel Goldwyn once said, "An oral agreement isn't worth the paper it's written on." He was correct. It would be nice if a borrower and a banker could consummate a transaction with a handshake, but that is not possible. Banking is an industry of red tape and paperwork, the latter required by common law and federal and state statutes. A banker who doesn't carefully prepare lending documents and have them properly signed soon will be out beating the bricks, looking for another job.

To discuss all the fine points in the lending documents in the bank's file cabinets would be a sure cure for insomnia; however, it is important that you have a broad overview of the documents that you will be signing. The examples I give will might not be identical to the papers you will sign but they are similar and serve the same purpose.

Lending Documents

The Promissory Note

The most important document is the *promissory note,* often referred to simply as *the note.* It represents a written contract between the borrower and the bank. The promissory note provides evidence of the debt.

The note specifies:

- The loan amount.
- The interest rate.
- The date the customer signed the note.
- The maturity date (the day the debt must be paid in full).
- The dates when any payments are due before the maturity date.
- Legal language stating that the customer promises to repay the bank.
- The customer's signature.

More than once a banker has had a customer sign the loan documents and then deposited money into the customer's checking account, only to discover after the borrower has left the bank that the note is missing a signature. Fortunately for banks, seldom does a loss result. In such a case, the banker places a hold on the funds (so the money can't be taken out of the account) until the customer comes back into the bank to sign the note. When this happens, usually the banker has a red face.

Certificate of Assumed Name, Partnership Borrowing Agreement, and Corporate Resolution to Borrow

If Merlyn Hemphill borrows as an individual, he signs a note with his name. If he borrows under a company name, such as Merlyn's Pro Golf Shop, a document that states that Merlyn Hemphill is the owner of a company called Merlyn's Pro Golf Shop must be included with the loan papers. If the company is operated as a sole proprietorship, some states use a form called a *certificate of assumed name,* which states that Merlyn Hemphill and Merlyn's Pro Golf Shop are one and the same.

If Merlyn is operating his company as either a partnership or a corporation, the bank will require a slightly different type of document. This document outlines who may borrow on behalf of the company. If the company is operating as a partnership, the form used is a *partnership borrowing agreement.* If the company is a corporation, the document is a *corporate resolution to borrow.*

Guaranties

With sole proprietorships and partnerships, the owner or owners are personally liable for the debts of their businesses. This is not the case for corporations. Should a corporation have financial problems and go into bankruptcy, unsecured creditors often do not collect the money owed to them. Unsecured creditors cannot rely on the personal resources of the corporation's stockholders for repayment.

A banker who loans money to a corporation wants to make sure the money will be repaid. It's common for bankers to require major stockholders to guarantee personally the loans to the corporation. If the company runs into financial problems, the stockholders are liable for the corporation's debts to the bank.

Guaranties can take one of two forms: general or limited. A *general guaranty* means the guarantor (the person making the guaranty) will stand behind all loans or credit lines made to a certain corporation or person. By comparison, a *limited guaranty* indicates the guarantor will stand behind debts to the bank up to a given amount. For instance, if the limited guaranty is for $20,000, the guarantor would be liable for only that amount.

Security Agreements

A *security agreement* is a legal document that states certain assets are assigned to the bank. If the customer doesn't make the loan payments, the bank has the right to take possession of the collateral, sell it, and use the proceeds to reduce the amount owed the bank.

UCC Financing Statements

Even with a secured loan, a bank can run a risk. Consider this scenario: Wally pledges his inventory as collateral to United National for his loan. Then he goes down the street and tries to use the same inventory for a loan with American National. Clearly Wally is dishonest, but how will United National and American National find out what he's trying to pull? Banks and other creditors must be able to determine if assets are currently pledged to other creditors.

The Uniform Commercial Code (UCC) meets this need. When certain types of assets are pledged, a document called a *UCC financing statement* is sent to an appropriate state agency. When it is officially filed, all interested parties are on notice that a particular asset has been pledged to a creditor.

Banks use UCC financing statements when the collateral is inventory, accounts receivable, equipment, fixtures, and the like—types of assets that do not have titles. With other types of collateral, such as vehicles (automobiles), airplanes, and ships, UCC financing statements do not apply. Instead the bank files an appropriate document with the federal or state agency recording the title to the property.

Term Loan Agreements

Depending on the policies of the bank, term loan agreements can be very broad or quite specific. These papers can be as simple as a letter signed by the borrower or as complex as a thick document drawn up by the bank's attorneys. More frequently it is a standardized form, and the banker simply fills in some or all of the appropriate blanks.

The agreement outlines the borrower's obligation—what he will and will not do. Sometimes bankers use affirmative or negative covenants to control the borrower further. *Affirmative covenants* are acts that borrowers agree to perform. *Negative covenants* restrict business owners from taking certain actions.

For instance: John Nye recently graduated from medical school and decided to establish a practice. After completing a written loan proposal, he approached a banker and outlined his need to borrow $125,000 to meet expenses associated with establishing his practice.

John's cash budget showed that he would be able to repay the bank's debt in five years. Because the cash flow of the practice would be tight in the first couple of years, initially he wanted to have reasonably low payments. Then, as the practice became more established, John would increase the payments accordingly. The banker agreed to the loan request provided John signed a loan agreement with the following covenants:

Working Capital

- The working capital position for the practice will not at any time be lower than $10,000.

Submission of Financial Reports

- Quarterly profit and loss statements will be provided to the bank within 30 days of the end of the quarter.
- Fiscal year-end financial statements will be provided to the bank within 60 days of the end of the fiscal year.

Compensation

- Withdrawals from the practice by the borrower for personal and household expenses will not exceed:

Fiscal Year	*Amount*
1	$40,000
2	$45,000
3	$50,000
4	No restriction
5	No restriction

Asset Acquisition

- Fixed assets above the purchase price of $10,000 will not be acquired without the bank's approval.

Compensating Balances

- A balance of $5,000 or more will be maintained in the practice's checking account at all times.

Additional Indebtedness

- The borrower will not incur additional indebtedness from another financial institution without the bank's approval.

Usually covenants are based on common sense and are designed to ensure that a business owner doesn't jeopardize the company's financial health—and the bank's repayment. Occasionally, however, a banker will suggest covenants that are unrealistic and don't allow the company owner enough room to maneuver.

Be sure you discuss any concerns with your banker before signing a term loan agreement. If you think a particular requirement is unworkable, say so and explain why. Most of the time a banker will agree to change a covenant if the owner makes a convincing case. After all, it's in the banker's best interest for your company to be successful.

As with any other legal transaction, always keep a copy of all signed documents.

The Final Processing

Once you leave the bank, papers in hand and money in your account, the banker still has work to do. Although you don't need to understand everything the loan officer does to finish processing your loan, some of the documents can affect you, so a little knowledge can be useful.

Credit Comments

Once the loan is made, your banker writes an in-house report, called a *credit comment.* The format of the report varies from bank to bank, but generally most credit comments contain the following sections:

- *Authorization:* Amount of your loan or credit line, interest rate, and terms of repayment.
- *Nature of business:* Your business organization, when established, summary of products and services, and future plans.
- *Management:* The banker's evaluation of your management team and its track record.
- *Purpose of loan:* Why you are borrowing the money.
- *Repayment sources:* A crucial section that covers your primary and alternative sources of repayment.
- *Collateral:* What asset(s) you have pledged as collateral and the value.

- *Documentation:* A listing of all the documents you have signed.
- *Financial statement analysis:* The bankers's analysis of your company and comparisons with other firms in the same industry.
- *Banking relationship:* A statement noting the average balance in your accounts and the length of time your company has done business with the bank.
- *General comment:* A summary.

The credit comment differs from some of the other documents I've discussed in one very important way: It is the private property of the bank. In almost all cases, the customer will never see the credit comment written about his or her loan.

Why should you care what the banker writes? Well, let's consider this scenario: Your banker asks you a question. Later he notes the answer in the credit comment. Weeks or even months later, he asks you the same question and compares your answer with that given previously. The question itself may not be of much importance, but the answer is. The loan officer is trying to assess how honest and straightforward you, the customer, are.

Senior bank officials and bank examiners routinely review credit comments and loan papers to make sure the loans fit the bank's guidelines and policies. And it's common for these reviewers to assign grades to the loans, as follows:

Grade A. Excellent loans and credit lines made to individuals or companies with unquestionable character. The financial position of borrowers is very strong. Collateral, if taken, is solid and of stable value. The companies are highly regarded in their industries and the community. The firms are liquid, and their ratios are well above the norm. The risk to the bank is minimal, and the handling costs are low.

Grade B. Desirable loans and credit lines made to borrowers of high personal integrity and backed by strong financial statements. It's highly unlikely that the companies will experience serious financial deterioration. The loans and lines granted have both a sound primary repayment source and a secondary means of repayment. It's expected the loans will be repaid in a reasonable period of time.

Grade C. Satisfactory loans and credit lines to borrowers of average financial strength. The borrowers might be subject to some vulnerability due to a major change in economic or industry conditions. The individuals' or companies' liquidity is within acceptable norms. Although the collateral used for secured loans provides adequate protection, it probably is not liquid.

Grade D. Loans and credit lines with one or more deficiencies that cannot be tolerated over the long term. Key financial ratios have deteriorated or show less-than-favorable trends. Immediate attention is needed to correct these concerns. The individuals or companies have limited liquidity.

Grade E. Loans and credit lines to individuals or companies that reflect a severe deterioration of financial condition. No immediate relief is in sight. The borrowers are unable to adjust to unfavorable economic or industry conditions. Unless the financial affairs of the borrowers improve considerably in the near term, a loss to the bank is probable.

Grade F. Loans and credit lines requiring immediate and drastic action or a loss to the bank is certain. The repayment sources are highly questionable. Selling the collateral would not result in sufficient funds to repay the bank's debt in full.

Bankers solicit loans only in the A, B, and C categories. But things change—sometimes for the worse. A grade A company may find itself reduced to a D because of some poor management decisions.

Several government agencies regulate the banking community. The effect these regulators have on you, the business owner, is significant, although it may appear distant. Government bank examiners routinely monitor financial institutions and the loans they make. Loans that in the opinion of the examiners have higher than acceptable risk are criticized. If a bank has a proportionally high number of criticized loans, the regulatory agency officials put pressure on the bank's managers to take appropriate actions so the depositors' money is protected. The agency officials also increase their supervision of the bank.

The lower the grade is on your loan, the more pressure bank management will put on the lending officer to protect the depositors' money. (We talk more about repayment problems in the next chapter.)

CHAPTER 15

If You Can't Repay the Bank . . .

Over the years I've had many telephone calls that start out: "Roger, do you have a minute? I'm having problems with my banker . . ." When that happens, I know that I should lean back and put my feet up . . . because it's going to be a long conversation.

Bob Bullis, a friend of a friend, recently called me. Bob is the owner of Bullis' Equipment, a heavy equipment company that rents backhoes, graders, loaders, and similar types of equipment.

Bob's problems started a couple of months ago when his bank contacted him because of an overdraft. He was perplexed. At the time, he said to his wife, "How can there be an overdraft? There is plenty of money in the checking account." The next day he learned the reason for the overdraft: His bookkeeper had been dipping into the till. After an audit by his accounting firm, Bob learned she had embezzled over $85,000 to support her drug habit.

Bob has major problems. As is usually the case, the police say Bob's chances of recovery from the bookkeeper are slim because she is practically penniless. He thought he had plenty of money to pay his bills, but he was wrong. Instead of a cash surplus, he has a big cash deficit. The bank and his suppliers are sympathetic to his situation, but they still want their money.

Bob says his banker is particularly hard to deal with since he feels a loss to the bank is likely. What is Bob going to do?

Agnes Wilson is president and chief executive officer of Pacific Health Clubs, which owns and operates recreational health clubs. Pacific Health Clubs sells annual memberships to people, who then use the club's athletic facilities.

Last year Pacific Health Clubs made a mistake: It expanded too fast by opening three new outlets. So far this year, revenues are not keeping up with projections. To make matters worse, recently there has been some negative publicity by the press as to "high-pressure" sales techniques used by some salespeople in the industry. Sales to new members have dropped off considerably for Pacific Health Clubs, and morale is bad. Agnes's cash flow is extremely tight, and she is unable to make her $18,000 monthly payments to the bank. What are her options? She must talk to her banker to find out.

Open Communications: An Essential Key to Solving Financial Problems

If you want a good relationship with your banker, be sure to maintain open communications. *This is especially true if you are having financial problems.*

It's natural to want to avoid your banker when you're having financial problems, but doing so can cost you time and money. In fact, avoiding your banker during troubled times can backfire. If you refuse to return your loan officer's calls, the result will be an aggravated and frustrated banker. If your loan is past due, it's only natural for a banker to think the worst and to focus on how to minimize the bank's losses. By not communicating with your loan officer, you encourage him to think the worst and proceed accordingly—perhaps calling for payment in full if the loan is past due or forcing you to sell your collateral. A banker forced by your silence to take such measures will not be tremendously receptive to working with you toward a less drastic solution.

In contrast, when you *initiate* a conversation about your money problems, you are taking the lead, showing you're on top of things, aware and in control. You're playing offense on the financial field. *The earlier you begin such discussions, the better your changes are of developing a repayment plan that works for you.*

Developing a Plan for Repayment

Before you create a workable plan for repayment, consider your banker's point of view. When faced with problem situations, bankers must ask themselves some tough questions:

- What is the earning outlook in the near future?
- Is it probable—or even possible—that the company will even earn enough profit to repay the bank?
- Can the borrower pledge additional collateral to protect the bank?
- Which assets could be sold to generate cash to repay the bank?

In this difficult situation, it's crucial for you to realize that the action taken by the bank depends on how the lending officer and supervisors view your financial situation: as getting worse, remaining the same, or improving.

When I was a loan officer supervisor, many times I heard my assistants say, "Maybe if we give it a little more time." Sometimes this is the right course of action. Other times it is not. It all depends on the financial outlook of the company involved.

A Stable or Improving Outlook

If your financial situation is likely to remain the same or improve, it's logical for your banker to *term out the debt.* This means you will be asked to make relatively small payments on a regular basis. This arrangement extends the length of time you have to repay the loan.

Optics, Inc., is a manufacturer of fashion frames, sports eyewear, and sunglasses. The firm distributes its product through major wholesalers around the country. In addition, Optics, Inc., is the main supplier to Twenty-Twenty Eyeware, an optical company with over 150 retail outlets in southern California.

The firm was founded in 1968 and operated by two partners, Carl Phillipp and Larry Lambert. Each partner owned 50 percent of the business. The managerial responsibilities were divided so Carl handled the marketing side of the business and Larry the operations.

Three years ago, Carl passed away from a massive heart attack. His death came as a complete surprise. In fact, he had had a checkup only two months before the attack and had passed it with flying colors.

Under terms of the partner's buy-sell agreement, if one owner died, the survivor would assume full responsibility for running the company. Thus, Larry took over running the marketing side of the business in addition to his existing duties.

The firm had been reasonably successful, but after Carl's death, the financial situation quickly deteriorated. The year after Carl's death, the company lost $38,000. The next year was even worse; the company lost $63,000. The third year after Carl's death, business improved, but the company still lost $28,000. With these sizable losses, the cash flow for Optics, Inc., became very tight. The company owed the bank $312,000 for the purchase of some injection-molding equipment. This debt is being repaid at the amount of $10,000 each month. Because of the severity of the losses, the company does not have enough cash to make the monthly payments to the bank.

When meeting with his banker, Larry outlines why he thinks the company has lost so much money over the last three years:

- Ed Norton, the company's best sales representative, quit and went to work for the competition. Not only has the transition hurt the company's sales, but several orders Optics expected to receive are now being filled by Ed's new company.
- The company made some poor choices in the selection of frames to manufacture. The fashion frame business is very trendy, and some of the frames Optics manufactured are not popular with consumers.

- With the company's oversupply of fashion frames and sports eyewear, Larry has had to reduce prices dramatically to sell this slow-moving inventory.
- With Carl's death, Larry also has had to manage the marketing side of the company. He is inexperienced in this area and has made some mistakes.

Larry also outlines the actions he has taken to address these concerns and why he expects the company to be profitable in the future:

- Jan Kenrud, a new sales representative, has been trained and has taken over Ed's accounts. Jan appears to be capable, and her sales record so far has been excellent.
- Rite and Associates, a marketing firm in New York that specializes in trends in the eyewear industry, has been retained by the firm. Rite has an excellent track record and will advise the company about the types of frames it should manufacture in the future.
- The out-of-style frame inventory has been liquidated. Frames now being produced will be sold at higher prices, which will result in a profit for the company.
- Larry has learned a great deal about the marketing of eyewear over the last three years. The losses were painful, but he feels the process has been educational. Larry thinks the company has turned the corner and that its future is bright.

From the banker's viewpoint, the Optics situation is like a bad news–good news joke. The bad news is that the company made some mistakes and suffered major financial losses. The good news is that the owner, Larry Lambert, appears to have identified the reasons and taken appropriate corrective action. Larry's logic makes sense.

The financial health of Optics is not good, but the situation appears to be stable, and perhaps even improving. The main problem is the company's cash flow: The company doesn't have the cash resources to make its monthly payment to the bank. Larry has prepared a cash budget that shows the company is able to make monthly payments of $6,000 to the bank.

After reviewing the situation, the banker agrees to change the repayment schedule and accept a $6,000 monthly payment. His options are limited. As always, the banker's first concern is having the debt repaid. If he does not agree to lower the monthly repayment terms, the company probably will be forced out of business. From the banker's perspective, it's much better to accept a lower payment over a longer period of time than to have Optics close its doors.

A revised repayment program, such as Optics's, is a little like eating an elephant—it takes a long time; however, bite by bite, progress is made. With each payment made, the amount owed is reduced. Even if it takes years, the debts eventually will be repaid. If Optics has any assets not pledged to another creditor, the bank probably will take a lien against them. A banker wants more collateral in case the financial situation worsens.

The lending officer will closely monitor the financial affairs of the company. To make sure he does his job, bank managers will require the lending officer to regularly submit reports on the progress being made.

A Bleak Outlook

Sometimes the banker and supervisors assess the situation as bad and getting worse; it's only a matter of time before the company fails. Sometimes a borrower will share this point of view, but more frequently a business owner will disagree. Many times, the owner hopes that with more time and with some additional money, everything will work out. Sometimes, however, the downward spiral continues, and Optics is a case in point.

The bank had lowered the monthly payment, and Larry, the owner, felt the company's situation was improving. But several months later, the situation went from bad to worse. Twenty-Twenty Eyeware, the company's largest account, terminated its relationship with Optics because it could acquire frames from another manufacturer at more competitive prices.

Now Optics was going to suffer another major loss—probably in the range of $60,000 to $100,000. The financial condition of the company could not withstand another setback. Without the revenues from Twenty-Twenty Eyeware, the company could not make its reduced monthly payments to the bank. Equally important, replacing the revenues generated by an account the size of Twenty-Twenty would be difficult, if not impossible. In the bank's opinion, the future for Optics was dismal; there was no light at the end of the tunnel. After reviewing the facts and options with his banker, Larry decided to close his doors. The assets were liquidated to pay off the bank and other creditors.

Selling the assets pledged as collateral is the most logical solution in such a situation. Most of the time a borrower is in a better position than the banker to sell assets because the owner knows the market and interested competitors who might want to buy the collateral. For bankers, however, liquidation is a distasteful and difficult task. Besides, the banker's primary interest is a quick sale. With each day that passes, the banker is confronted with two expenses: the interest earned on the business owner's debt and the cost of bank personnel trying to find a buyer for the collateral.

The value of collateral can disappear almost as fast as Houdini did in front of an audience. Frequently used equipment and other assets sell for only a fraction of what an owner thinks it is worth. I've seen inventory sold for as low as 25 to 30 cents on the dollar. Sometimes the collection of accounts receivable can yield even more disappointing results. When a financial institution collects the accounts receivable of a firm, the debtors come up with thousands of reasons why they should not be required to pay their bills. The merchandise was the incorrect size, the wrong color, damaged in shipment, or some other reason. Some people who owe money can be amazingly creative when inventing reasons for nonpayment.

I do not exaggerate when I tell you that I could fill this entire book with horror stories about banks selling collateral. And that's why I encourage anyone faced with selling collateral to work with his banker. In almost all cases, the business owner knows the marketplace better than anyone working for the bank and can best dispose of the collateral.

Still, borrowers are usually disappointed with the amount of money raised by the sale of their assets. Sometimes bankers are unpleasantly surprised too.

In one case, a banker loaned $125,000 to a radio station to purchase equipment that cost $175,000. The bank felt they had an adequate margin should financial problems develop. A year later, the station's management made some poor decisions and began having financial difficulties. Bankruptcy soon followed.

When the bank tried to liquidate the collateral, it learned that much of the equipment was custom made and constructed especially for the station. It operated only at the frequency transmitted by that station. None of the other stations in the area could use any of the equipment because it wouldn't work at the frequency they transmitted. The bank lost over $100,000 in this situation.

In another case, Rodney, a loyal employee, was fired after expressing a difference of opinion with Walter, the owner of the company. Walter felt he was always right, so anyone with a differing opinion had to be wrong. It's not surprising that Walter frequently had conflicts with others.

Some months later, his company started having financial problems, and the situation deteriorated rapidly. Walter and the bank made the joint decision to close the doors and hold an auction. The money raised from the sale of the company's assets would pay off the creditors.

One asset being sold was the owner's office furniture, his pride and joy. He had paid over $4,000 for his imported rosewood desk, executive chair, and credenza. The successful bidder of the office equipment was Rodney, the ex-employee. He paid $480 for his boss's furnishings and went away with a smile.

If Money From the Sale of the Collateral Doesn't Equal the Amount Owed the Bank

Some borrowers believe that if they cannot repay the bank, the financial institution simply takes the collateral and forgives the obligation. Then each party goes merrily on his way. This is NOT true. Borrowers have a legal obligation to pay the *entire* amount of the debt.

Elmer Edwards, the owner of a sporting goods store, owes the bank $80,000. The collateral is sold for net proceeds of

$70,000. Elmer is still liable for $10,000. Not only that, but the bank wants cash for this remaining amount. The bankers will not be satisfied with accepting Elmer's equity in his limited partnership, which owns property off the coast of Cuba. Nor are they interested in accepting his autographed picture of Babe Ruth or his priceless rubber duck collection for the remaining balance. Elmer must raise $10,000 in cash to pay off the balance of the loan. If he doesn't, the bankers will wait until his finances improve and then go after the money.

To put a rosier glow on this case, should the sale of Elmer's collateral net $85,000, $80,000 would go to the bank, and he would get to keep the extra $5,000.

Bankers almost always regard "debts *plus interest* must be paid in full" as a rule not to be broken. The only exception is if there are rare extenuating circumstances. For example, a business venture was established by four partners. Each owned an equal share of the business. Several years later, Bruce, one of the partners, ran into financial difficulty. He eventually terminated his relationship with the others and was on the verge of personal bankruptcy. At the time of his termination, he owed the bank $65,000. His only assets were a small amount of equity in his house and his portion of the company's retirement program. Both assets are protected under the bankruptcy laws.

Bruce approached his former partners and arranged an early cash settlement on his retirement program of $30,000. Next, he approached his banker with the desire to avoid bankruptcy. Yet he did not have a job, the outlook was not bright, and he had no money to pay the bank.

He informed the banker of his situation. He also explained that according to his attorney, both his retirement program and the equity in his house were protected under the bankruptcy laws. He told his banker, however, that he was willing to accept the early cash settlement of $30,000. Then he would give this amount of money to the bank, providing it would accept this amount as payment in full. In other words, the bank would receive $30,000 rather than the $65,000 owed.

The program Bruce outlined had advantages for him and the bank: He could avoid bankruptcy, and the bank would receive a portion of the money owed. It thus allowed the bank to limit its losses. The bank officers agreed to Bruce's offer.

The circumstances regarding this situation were unique, however. If Bruce did not have the option of bankruptcy, the bank would not have agreed to his proposal. It would have waited. It knew that he would have gone back to work sooner or later and had a regular income. Then the bank would take appropriate legal action. Over time it would collect the entire amount of money owed *plus* accrued interest.

Also, if Bruce had given the bank the retirement money and then attempted to negotiate, it would have been a different story. In this case, Bruce would not have had any bargaining power. Once again, the bank would have simply waited. And each day while it waited, interest would accrue on the debt. Once Bruce was back on his feet and had a monthly income, the bank would demand its money.

In summary, one of my bosses told me, "Preventing loan problems is always better than correcting loan problems." That's true for both the borrower and the banker. The best way to prevent problems is with financial planning, maintaining open communications with your banker, and having a viable alternative course of action in case your plans do not work out as expected.

When you borrow money from a bank, remember that you and the bank have a legal, enforceable agreement—and don't expect the bank to make exceptions. Mark Twain once said, "A banker is a fellow who lends you his umbrella when the sun is shining and wants it back the minute it begins to rain." I think Twain must have known a lot of bankers.

CHAPTER 16

The ABC's of SBA Loans

Bob Mayes owns and operates a deli-style bakery and coffee shop known as Mayes' Haven. The deli, located in the downtown business district, is open from 6 A.M. to 5 P.M., Monday through Friday. Bob's customers are mainly businesspeople who work downtown. Mayes' Haven specializes in gourmet sandwiches and delicious pastries.

Bob, age 39, founded his company five years ago. Prior to establishing Mayes' Haven, he spent nine years as a restaurant manager with the Hilton Hotel chain.

Because of Bob's managerial skills and outgoing personality, his company has prospered. The food is great, the deli's atmosphere is pleasant, and Bob makes every customer feel at home. Each year, his sales and profits have increased.

Riley Richardson also is in the restaurant business. He owns and operates two successful sandwich shops in another part of the downtown core. Riley is in ill health and, upon the advice of his doctor, has decided to sell his business. Riley contacted Bob and offered to sell the two sandwich shops for a cash price of $200,000.

After reviewing the records of the sandwich shops, Bob thinks Riley's asking price is reasonable. Both outlets benefit from an excellent location, a solid clientele, and only a limited amount of competition in the immediate vicinity. Since Bob would like to expand, he thinks it makes sense to acquire Riley's two shops.

After reviewing his financial resources and preparing a loan proposal, Bob approaches his banker for a $160,000 term loan, the amount he needs to borrow in order to acquire Riley's business.

When presented with the loan request, Bob's banker perceives some pluses and minuses. On the plus side:

- Over the past five years, Bob has proved he is a capable and successful restaurateur.
- The asking price of Riley's sandwich shops appears to be reasonable.
- Acquiring the two shops would be a natural expansion step for Bob.
- Bob has roughly $70,000 of his own money to put into the project. Of this amount, $40,000 (plus the bank loan) will go to Riley. The remaining $30,000 will be used for leasehold improvements, new signs, and miscellaneous expenses associated with converting the shops to new Mayes' Havens.

On the negative side, Bob's banker thinks:

- Much of the $200,000 asking price represents acquiring the rights to Riley's two locations, customer base, and overall favorable reputation. The actual market value of the used restaurant equipment and other physical assets is probably not over $40,000.
- Bob has limited financial strength. Other than $70,000 in cash, his only other significant assets are some equity in his home and his business. Not only that, but trying to place a value on his business is difficult. While the deli provides him with a good living, its success is directly attributed to Bob's capabilities. If something should happen to Bob, the value of his firm would be questionable.
- Future profits represent the primary repayment source. If profits are not sufficient to repay the bank, Bob does not have a viable secondary repayment source.

Bob's banker has some concerns. Bob's financial strength is limited. If he can't make enough profits to repay the bank, the bank could lose money. For these reasons, it's likely that the banker will turn down Bob's loan request.

Bob's request is typical of many other financing requests. At first glance, it makes sense; however, from a banker's perspective, there is too much risk. This degree of risk could be caused by a number of factors. Maybe the entrepreneur is short on managerial experience. Perhaps he or she doesn't have quite enough money to put into the business. Or maybe, like Bob, the business owner's financial strength is on the light side. A banker who sees more minuses than pluses will pass on the opportunity to participate in a business venture.

Perhaps, however, someone (or an organization) with solid financial strength is willing to stand behind or guarantee the loan request. Then if the borrower is not able to make the payments to the bank, this other party would be responsible. In such a case, the banker would have a very different attitude. With considerably less risk to the financial institution, the banker frequently will give the business owner the money needed.

That's the primary role of the Small Business Administration (SBA). It partially guarantees loans made by banks to the business community. Financing requests that are basically sound but represent too great a risk to the banker can be approved with an SBA guarantee.

Congress created the SBA in 1953. The term *small business* is actually somewhat of a misnomer, since, according to SBA standards, about 99 percent of the 15.2 million nonfarm businesses in the United States fit into the agency's definition of "small business." Together these businesses account for more than half of all private employment and nearly half of all goods and services produced each year.

Today the SBA has approximately 3,700 permanent employees and over 100 offices across the country. It offers a variety of services (which I'll discuss later) but is best known for its guaranteed bank loan program.

SBA Guaranteed Loan Program

If you, the borrower, cannot or do not make your loan payments, the SBA will pay the bank a percentage of the amount owed.

The percentage varies, but it's common for the SBA to guarantee up to 90 percent of the amount owed the bank.

A business owner can use the loan proceeds to meet a variety of needs, such as increasing working capital, acquiring equipment, or purchasing facilities. On occasion, borrowers may even use the loan proceeds to consolidate their outstanding debts.

The maximum amount of money that the SBA will guarantee is $500,000. Depending on the situation, repayment can occur over a period of time as long as 25 years. Money borrowed to increase a company's working capital is usually repaid within seven years. The average size of a guaranteed loan is about $175,000 and the average maturity date about eight years. The interest rate on SBA loans is usually 2¼ or 2¾ percent above the bank's prime rate.

Most businesses are eligible for an SBA guaranteed loan; however, the SBA is *forbidden* to guarantee a loan if any of the following conditions exists:

- The loan proceeds are otherwise available on reasonable terms.

  Example: First American Bank has offered to grant Dick Flowers's loan request and has quoted an interest rate of its prime rate plus 3 percent. Dick suggests borrowing the money through the SBA guaranteed loan program because the interest rate is lower.

- The loan proceeds are to be used to pay off creditors who are inadequately secured.

  Example: DeAnne Ottaway, owner of a drapery business, owes two major creditors $240,000, which is inadequately secured. DeAnne wants to apply for an SBA loan to pay them off.

- The loan proceeds are for speculation or investment purposes.

  Example: Duke Campbell wants to borrow $205,000 under the SBA's guaranteed loan program to buy an eight-unit apartment building.

- The applicant is a newspaper, magazine, book publisher, movie theater, or nonprofit enterprise (except sheltered workshops).

  Example: Don Kent, publisher of Kent's Newspaper, wants to borrow $125,000 to improve the newspaper's working capital position.

- The applicant is too large under the SBA's criteria.

  Example: Emory Thurnau, owner of Thurnau's Manufacturing, Inc., which employs 604 people, wants to borrow $350,000 to expand plant and facilities. (For manufacturers, SBA rules require fewer than 500 employees.)

None of the applicants in the foregoing examples meets SBA guidelines; all their proposals would be rejected.

Using the SBA Program

Select a bank and make an application for a loan in the usual manner. If your banker decides to give you the money, congratulations! You don't need—and probably won't hear about—the SBA guaranteed loan program. If the banker has no interest in your project, your request for funds will be turned down.

Sometimes, however, the banker is interested in making the loan provided the SBA guarantees a major portion of the debt. In such a case, the banker will forward the written loan proposal, SBA application, and his own comments to the agency. (In the vast majority of cases, most of the communication is between the SBA and the bank.) SBA lending officers then review the material and decide whether to guarantee the loan. The SBA's decision depends on the banker's comments, the SBA application, and the loan proposal package. When reviewing the loan package, SBA personnel focus on the financial projections, the owner's managerial abilities, and the amount of the owner's equity in the company.

The main difference between the SBA and the bank in lending money is that the SBA has slightly more lenient guidelines. The written proposal needs to make sense (and to follow the points I outline in Chapter 10). The SBA isn't interested in giving tax dollars to an ambitious entrepreneur looking for a handout.

SBA lending officers look at the financial projections in the same manner as bankers do. They place particular emphasis on the cash budget because they want to make sure the applicant will have enough money to meet the firm's expenses, the owner's draw, and payments to the bank. If the cash flow situation doesn't look good, the SBA officials will refuse the request.

The SBA takes on the more challenging task of assessing the owner's managerial abilities. Reviewing officers place heavy emphasis on the owner's track record. If you are starting a new venture, the SBA will cast a critical eye on your résumé. Reviewers want to see some background in a similar type of business, along with some managerial experience—preferably in the same type of product or service.

The SBA's desire for owners to have some management experience is based on statistics. Studies show that of all new businesses established, about one third will be out of business within a year. By the end of the second year, roughly half will have closed their doors. By the fifth year, over two thirds of the companies will be history. There are many reasons why businesses fail; however, study after study has shown the number one reason for businesses going under is poor management.

SBA reviewing officers also consider the amount of the owner's equity in a company. With new businesses, the SBA reviewing officer wants a business owner to have about 50 cents of equity in the business for every dollar of projected liabilities (a debt-to-worth ratio of not greater than 2.0).

Vicki Van Houtte is establishing a company that will distribute an upscale line of umbrellas to exclusive specialty stores around the country. After obtaining a $90,000 SBA loan, Vicki estimates her company's financial picture will look like this:

VVH Umbrellas, Inc.
Pro Forma Balance Sheet

Current assets	$120,000	Current liabilities	$ 60,000
Fixed assets	155,000	Fixed liabilities	120,000
		Total Liabilities	$180,000
		NET WORTH	95,000
TOTAL ASSETS	$275,000	AND NET WORTH	$275,000

She then determines her debt-to-worth ratio:

$$\frac{\text{Total debt}}{\text{Net worth}} = \frac{\$180,000}{\$95,000} = 1.89$$

Vicki's request is within the SBA's guidelines, since, assuming her SBA loan goes through, her debt-to-worth ratio is 2.0 or less.

The SBA takes a more lenient approach toward existing businesses since the company's track record is a ready source of information. Here the SBA's rule of thumb is for business owners to have at least 25 cents of equity for every dollar of liabilities (a debt-to-worth ratio of not greater than 4.0).

A well-organized and impressive written loan proposal is essential for the approval of an SBA-guaranteed loan. Most of the time, you won't even meet with any SBA lending officers, so your proposal must be convincing. The SBA's decision to guarantee your loan depends on your banker's comments, the SBA application, and the loan proposal package.

Banks and the SBA: A Major Difference

When deciding to guarantee a loan, the SBA places less emphasis on collateral than do most bankers. Traditionally, collateral has been only a minor concern of the SBA, especially when compared to the financial projections, owner's managerial abilities, and the amount of the owner's equity in the company. When the SBA guarantees a loan, however, it usually requires that all unencumbered company assets be pledged as collateral. It is also common for the SBA to ask business owners to pledge personal assets, even including such items as a second mortgage on the owner's home. The SBA wants to lend to business owners who are committed—financially and otherwise—to making their companies a success.

Other SBA Programs

Although the guaranteed loan program is the SBA's major service, it offers other programs too. Best known are its direct loan and SCORE programs.

Direct Loan Program

The SBA has a direct loan program, with the maximum amount advanced set at $150,000. Under this program, the would-be borrower applies directly to the SBA for financing. Like the bank-guaranteed program, the SBA will not grant a direct loan request if the money is otherwise available from banks. In fact, to be considered for the direct loan program, business owners must show that their request has been declined by a bank in the local community. This program is excellent, but the demand for the limited amount of available funds is high.

The Score Program: Benefit From Experience

The SBA's SCORE (Service Corps of Retired Executives) program matches retired executives with business owners that request the service. SCORE staff can help with everything from developing a business plan to establishing procedures for collecting accounts receivable.

SCORE staff members can provide insight and guidance based on their many years of experience—at no cost to the business owner. The SBA pays all costs associated with operating SCORE.

Figure 16-1. Summary of SBA guaranteed loan guidelines.

Credit Requirements

1. *Cash flow:* The cash budget needs to show the firm can pay all business expenses, the owner's draw, and payments to the bank.

2. *Management:* The borrower needs to show that he or she can successfully operate a business. If the applicant is operating an existing business, the SBA reviews the track record and profitability of the company.

An applicant starting a new business or buying a firm needs a managerial background and needs to demonstrate some experience in the industry he or she is entering.

3. *Equity capital:* Applicants need to have some of their own money in the business ventures. For an established firm, the rule of thumb after making the loan is $1 of owner's equity for every $4 of liabilities (debt-to-worth ratio of 4.0 or less).

For new business ventures or when the borrower is buying an existing firm, the guidelines are tougher: $1 of owner's equity for every $2 of liabilities (debt-to-worth ratio of 2.0 or less).

The SBA might require the business owner to pledge personal assets as collateral. However, the SBA does not consider these assets as equity in the company. Equity capital is the owner's net investment in the business.

Loan Amount

The SBA may guarantee up to 90 percent of an eligible bank loan. The maximum loan amount is $500,000.

Maturity

The maximum maturity is 25 years. Working capital loans usually do not exceed 7 years.

Interest Rate

The interest rate charged on loans that mature in 7 years or less is 2¼ percent over the bank's prime rate. For loans that mature in over 7 years, the normal interest rate is 2¾ percent over prime.

Customarily, the rate charged the borrower fluctuates as the prime rate goes up or down.

Fees

The borrower is usually charged an up-front fee of 2 percent of the loan amount. This is normally added to the loan amount to yield the total that is repaid over time.

Collateral

The SBA will probably take a lien against all available assets of the company. The SBA might also require liens against personal assets of the owner.

Size Standards

The size limits for SBA eligibility vary within specific industries. Approximate guidelines are:

- *Retailers:* Annual sales of less than $3.5 million.
- *Wholesalers:* Fewer than 500 employees.
- *Manufacturers:* Fewer than 500 employees.
- *General contractors:* Average annual receipts of $17 million or less.
- *Specialty contractors:* Average annual receipts of $7 million or less.
- *Farms:* Annual sales of $500,000 or less.

Eligibility

Most small businesses are eligible; however, the SBA is forbidden to make a loan if any of the following factors apply:

- A loan is available on otherwise reasonable terms.
- The company is larger than the size limits outlined above.
- The loan is to be used to pay off inadequately secured creditors.
- The loan is for speculative or investment purposes (e.g., to purchase rental property).
- The applicant is a newspaper, magazine, book publisher, movie theater, or nonprofit enterprise (except sheltered workshop).

How to Apply

1. Prepare a written loan proposal.
2. Apply for a conventional bank loan at a bank of your choice.
3. If the bank declines your request, ask if the bank will consider your request under the SBA's guaranteed loan program.
4. If the bank is willing to participate in the SBA's program, the lending officer will ask you to complete an SBA application.

5. The banker forwards the loan proposal, SBA application, and comments to the SBA for review.

The SBA has played a vital role in the health of American business. By providing financial backing and support, it has encouraged and assisted banks in making thousands of loans to the business community. The primary disadvantage to working with the SBA is the large amount of paperwork (no surprise, since this is a government agency). But the additional red tape is a small price to pay if you can satisfy your financial needs. A summary of the SBA guaranteed loan guidelines appears in Figure 16-1.

As with all other organizations, the SBA's guidelines change from time to time. To learn more about the guaranteed loan program or the other services offered by the Small Business Administration, contact the closest regional office or write:

Small Business Administration
1441 L Street Northwest
Washington, D.C. 20416

CHAPTER 17

The Seven Golden Rules for Dealing With Bankers

By now you're something of an expert about bankers. In teaching you how to borrow money from a banker, I've let you inside the mind of a typical lending officer. The more you understand about a banker's perspective, the better service you'll be able to obtain.

I offer you seven golden rules for dealing with bankers. Remember, these rules are designed to make your life easier—not necessarily to make the banker's life more golden. Actually your relationship with your banker can pay off for both of you.

Golden Rule 1: Never surprise your banker with bad news. Bankers don't like to be surprised. They want to understand fully the borrower's situation. That way they feel they are working with entrepreneurs rather than just trying to protect the deositors' money.

It's easy to keep bankers informed when everything is going well. Open communications, however, often stop as soon as a company starts having financial difficulty. The business owner hopes that the situation will improve and reasons that by not mentioning anything now, he or she will avoid an unpleasant confrontation.

What does the entrepreneur risk with this approach? Credibility. When the owner misses a payment and doesn't provide an explanation (and starts ignoring telephone calls), the banker's antenna goes up. He immediately becomes concerned about the (possible serious) problems the company is encountering.

I can't emphasize this rule enough: It's almost always better to be honest and tell the good *and* the bad. A banker is like a bloodhound and sooner or later will find you. The more the banker has to search, the worse his disposition and the less he is willing to accommodate you.

Golden Rule 2: Make your loan payments on time. Human nature being what it is, some people make their payments either early or on time. And, once again because of human nature, some people always seem to run late. Most bankers get a list of their past-due loans each day. Just as you'd expect, a banker keeps a close watch on this list. If you are going to run a few days late, it's wise to make a quick telephone call to the bank. All you have to do is tell your loan officer when to expect to receive payment. A quick telephone call can go a long way in helping to create a positive relationship.

Golden Rule 3: Provide accurate and timely financial information. Newspaper editors say, "Yesterday's news isn't worth reading." But in banking, yesterday's results are very important: Financial reports show a company's financial strength, profit picture, and, equally important, trends.

Financial reports are an essential tool bankers use to make lending decisions. Obviously, reports submitted that contain errors are distressing. When bankers find errors, they begin to doubt the accuracy of the reports and other information submitted. They want to know what is currently happening in businesses. As such, it's important to prepare and submit to bankers financial reports reasonably soon after the close of the accounting period.

Golden Rule 4: Invite your banker to visit your company. A good banking relationship is a continuing educational process—on both sides. As a borrower, you need continually to supply your banker with information about your abilities, your company, and your industry. The more the banker understands the total picture, the better he is able to serve your banking needs.

There's no substitute for a visit to your company. An occasional visit helps give your banker a real-world perspective.

Along this same line, once in a while, invite your banker to lunch. It gives you a chance to know each other a little better. And you both get away from the pillars of the financial institution.

Golden Rule 5: Never spend the money before you receive it. Frequently your banker does not have the authority to approve a loan request. When the dollar amount of the request is above the banker's lending limit authority, the loan proposal gets booted upstairs to the higher level of authority needed to approve it.

More than once a lending officer has said, "The loan looks good to me"—and has to eat these words when the customer's request is turned down by the loan committee. The banker may have a red face, but the customer is the one with the problem.

Do not take your banker's offhand comment as a firm commitment. Make commitments to spend the money after everything is signed and you have the funds in hand.

Golden Rule 6: Discuss important matters in person rather than over the telephone. When you want to negotiate details of a term loan agreement, ask for a lower rate, or discuss some other important point, do so in person rather than over the telephone. Not only will you be able to read the banker's body language, but you will have more time to explain your viewpoint and make your case.

Golden Rule 7: If you have a good banker, send him referrals. Competent professionals are worth their weight in gold. If you're dealing with a capable banker, refer your friends and business associates. He will appreciate your efforts, and so will your colleagues.

You and Your Banker

Not too many years ago, most bankers focused on their banks' policies and guidelines. It was an industry based on tradition and procedures rather than meeting the needs of their customers.

As one of my favorite customers said, "At one time, innovation in the banking industry was changing the teller line from many short lines to a long one." (This was the same guy who said, "Bankers represent a class society: 'sitters' and 'standers'.")

Those days are rapidly disappearing. With deregulation, banking has become a highly competitive industry, and the increased competition forces all banks to serve the needs of their customers better.

High-quality service is what you need and deserve to receive from your banker. If you are receiving it, that's great. If not, perhaps you should consider transferring your business to someone who truly wants it.

You need to have a capable banker—someone who is not only a consultant and a means of obtaining financial assistance but a valuable member of your management team.

How to Borrow Money From a Banker was written to teach you about the inner world of banking and how to deal with bankers. It is a guide and resource tool that shows you how to obtain the money you need to reach your financial goals.

I hope the information in this book will help you establish and maintain a good relationship with a competent banker—a banker who will provide you the quality of service that you deserve. If that is the case, I have been successful.

APPENDIX A

Sample Loan Proposal

Financial Proposal

for

HENRY'S TIRES AND SERVICE, INC.

submitted to:

SECOND NATIONAL BANK

Seattle, Washington

Henry Jay
20 South Auburn
Bellevue, WA 98025
(206) 555-8946

October 15, 19X5

October 15, 19X5

Second National Bank
Attn: Mr. Tom Friberg
Assistant Vice President
215 East Second Avenue
Seattle, WA 99336

Dear Mr. Friberg:

Enclosed is a financing request for Henry's Tires and Service, Inc., a retail distributor of tires, batteries, and related accessories. My company is established as a corporation and has been doing business in the state of Washington since 19X1.

This financing package is for two separate requests. First, I am seeking a line of credit in the amount of $75,000 to assist with the company's needs for additional inventory and accounts receivable during the busy late spring and summer seasons.

Second, a $20,000 term loan is being requested for the purchase of a new Ford truck.

Should you desire additional information, please contact me at (206) 555-8946. Thank you for your consideration.

Yours truly,

Henry Jay

Henry Jay
President

HJ:rba
enclosures

Table of Contents

AMOUNT AND USES OF LOAN PROCEEDS

1. $75,000 Credit Line

The busy season for the company starts during the late spring and continues into the summer. A credit line is being requested to cover the company's need for increased working capital (primarily additional inventory and accounts receivable) during this period.

2. $20,000 Term Loan

The company has a need for a new 1.5-ton truck to be used in the business.

A fully equipped vehicle, which has the compressor and other equipment needed to repair or replace large truck tires, can be purchased for $25,000. The firm wishes to make a down payment of $5,000 and finance the balance over two years.

HISTORY AND DESCRIPTION OF BUSINESS

Henry's Tire and Service, Inc., was established as a corporation under the laws of Washington in 19X1. The company has two retail outlets that serve the general public. The home office was opened in 19X1 and is located at 20 South Auburn, Bellevue, Washington. The second outlet was opened in 19X2 and is located at 4105 98th North East in Mountlake Terrace.

Henry's Tire and Service has continued to grow and prosper over the years. During the past year, the company had an opportunity to purchase an existing tire outlet in Redmond. Negotiations were held, but management ultimately decided that it did not want to expand at this time.

MANAGEMENT TEAM

Henry's Tire and Service was founded by Henry Jay, 58 years of age. He owns 80 percent of the outstanding common stock and is the president and chief executive officer of the company. Prior to the establishment of this company, he spent 16 years working for Goodyear Tire and Rubber. His last six years with that company were spent as a store manager.

Ron Jay, Henry's son, serves as secretary and treasurer of the company. He is 28 years old and owns 20 percent of the outstanding common stock. Ron has worked in the family-owned business since he was in high school. Upon obtaining his degree in physical education from Washington State University, he returned to Bellevue to work in the business on a full-time basis.

Henry has been the general manager of the Bellevue outlet since its inception. For the past four years, Ron has been responsible for managing the Mountlake Terrace facility. Policy decisions that affect the direction of the company are made jointly by the two Jays.

While the management functions are basically handled by these two individuals, each store has seasoned employees who can handle the operations of the stores in the absence of either of the two owners.

Henry plans to continue working for a number of years. When he does retire, it is expected that Ron will assume his duties as president and leader of the company.

PRODUCT/SERVICE INFORMATION

The two retail outlets offer a broad line of tire products, services, and related accessories. Their clientele are primarily people who live and work in the communities of Bellevue and Mountlake Terrace.

Both outlets have a similar product mix. Roughly 50 percent of total revenues is derived from the sale of tires; 30 percent from the service aspect of the company; and 10 percent from servicing three major accounts (Washington Water Works, Bentley County Public Utilities Department, and Puget Sound Trucking). The remaining 10 percent of the revenues comes from the sales of wheels, batteries, and other miscellaneous accessories.

The major line of tires carried by the company is the Fremont brand, which is manufactured in Taiwan. The product is comparable in quality to the Goodyear Maxi-mile and the Firestone Superplus tires. While the Fremont brand does not have the name familiarity of the major brands, Fremont is sold at a price 10 to 15 percent below the name-brand competition. Henry's has used the Fremont brand as its major line for the past seven years, and customer satisfaction has been excellent.

For customers who prefer a brand-name tire, the company also offers for sale a limited number of Bridgestone, B. F. Goodrich, and Cooper Tires. About 80 percent of tire sales comes from the Fremont brand, with the balance fairly equally divided among the other three manufacturers.

The service side of the company primarily performs the following functions: tire mounting, balancing, rotating, and flat tire services; and installation of wheels, shocks, and batteries.

For the past several years, the company has been the tire servicing company for Washington Water Works and the Bentley County PUD. Its contracts with these companies extend through 19X8 and 19X9, respectively. Recently a similar contract was signed with Puget Sound Trucking covering the next two years.

FINANCIAL STATEMENTS

Following are the fiscal year-end statements on the company covering the last three years. They were prepared by the accounting firm of Ulland and Manning, CPAs.

If for any reason you would like to contact Chuck Ulland or Johnny Manning, they can be reached at 555-7493. Both are familiar with the financial affairs of the business.

Henry's Tire and Service, Inc.
Balance Sheet
September 30, 19X5
($ in 000s)

Cash	$ 18
Accounts receivable	159
Inventory	350
Prepaid expenses	23
Total current assets	550
Equipment (net)	140
Other assets	25
TOTAL ASSETS	$715
Notes payable	$ 70
Accounts payable	265
Other current liabilities	10
Total current liabilities	345
Long-term debt	130
TOTAL LIABILITIES	$475
NET WORTH	$240
TOTAL LIABILITIES AND NET WORTH	$715

Henry's Tire and Service, Inc.
Income Statement
September 30, 19X5
($ in 000s)

Sales	$2,000
Cost of goods sold	1,240
Gross profit	760
Operating expenses	700
Operating profit	60
Other expenses	14
Before-tax profit	46
Income taxes	10
Net profit	$ 36

Henry's Tire and Service, Inc.
Balance Sheet
September 30, 19X4
($ in 000s)

Cash	$ 15
Accounts receivable	150
Inventory	260
Prepaid expenses	15
Total current assets	440
Equipment (net)	138
Other assets	34
TOTAL ASSETS	$612
Notes payable	$ 60
Accounts payable	206
Other current liabilities	9
Total current liabilities	275
Long-term debt	133
TOTAL LIABILITIES	$408
NET WORTH	$204
TOTAL LIABILITIES AND NET WORTH	$612

Henry's Tire and Service, Inc.
Income Statement
September 30, 19X4
($ in 000s)

Sales	$1,625
Cost of goods sold	1,005
Gross profit	620
Operating expenses	570
Operating profit	50
Other expenses	10
Before-tax profit	40
Income taxes	8
Net profit	$ 32

Henry's Tire and Service, Inc.
Balance Sheet
September 30, 19X3
($ in 000s)

Cash	$ 12
Accounts receivable	103
Inventory	255
Prepaid expenses	10
Total current assets	380
Equipment (net)	127
Other assets	25
TOTAL ASSETS	$532
Notes payable	$ 53
Accounts payable	168
Other current liabilities	4
Total current liabilities	225
Long-term debt	135
TOTAL LIABILITIES	360
NET WORTH	172
TOTAL LIABILITIES AND NET WORTH	$532

Henry's Tire and Service, Inc.
Income Statement
September 30, 19X3
($ in 000s)

Sales	$1,340
Cost of goods sold	835
Gross profit	505
Operating expenses	466
Operating profit	39
Other expenses	7
Before-tax profit	32
Income taxes	6
Net profit	$ 26

FINANCIAL PROJECTIONS

Following are a pro forma income statement, cash budget, and pro forma balance sheet for the fiscal year ending September 30, 19X6.

Sales for the year are expected to increase about 15 percent–from $2,000,000 in 19X5 to $2,300,00 in 19X6. It's anticipated this will result in an after-tax profit of $43,000.

The cash budget shows funds will be needed from the bank beginning in December. It's anticipated that the borrowings will peak in April at roughly $68,000, and by August the line should be paid off in full. Since the projections may understate the company's financial needs, a line of $75,000 is being requested.

The $20,000 loan to acquire the new truck will be needed in March, with payments commencing the following month.

The pro forma balance sheet as of September 30, 19X6, shows assets of $831,000, liabilities of $548,000, and a net worth of $283,000.

Monthly Pro Form Income Statement and Cash Budget
19X6
($ in 000s)

	Oct	Nov	Dec	Jan	Feb	Mar	Apr	May	Jun	Jul	Aug	Sep	Total
Sales	180	165	160	160	165	200	225	230	225	215	195	180	2,300
Cost of goods sold	111	102	98	99	102	125	140	142	140	134	121	111	1,425
Gross profit	69	63	62	61	63	75	85	88	85	81	74	69	875
Operating expenses	66	66	66	66	66	66	66	66	65	65	65	65	788
Depreciation	1	1	1	1	1	1	1	1	1	1	1	1	12
Total	67	67	67	67	67	67	67	67	66	66	66	66	800
Operating profit	2	(4)	(5)	(6)	(4)	8	18	21	19	15	8	3	75
Other income (expense)							(3)	(5)	(5)	(5)	(2)		(20)
Net profit before taxes	2	(4)	(5)	(6)	(4)	8	15	16	14	10	6	3	55

	Oct	Nov	Dec	Jan	Feb	Mar	Apr	May	Jun	Jul	Aug	Sep
CASH BUDGET												
Cash balance beginning	18	18	9	8	8	8	8	8	8	8	8	10
Plus receipts												
Cash sales	166	150	140	140	150	170	190	200	190	185	170	165
Accounts receivable collected	25	15	15	20	20	15	30	35	30	35	30	15
Bank (credit line)			16	12	4	33	3					
Bank loan						20						
Total cash available	209	183	180	180	182	246	231	243	228	228	208	190
Less disbursements												
Merchandise	82	72	70	70	72	90	95	97	95	91	88	78
Payroll	35	35	35	35	35	35	35	35	35	35	35	35
General and administrative expense	66	66	66	66	66	66	66	66	65	65	65	65
Base inventory increase						21	15	10				
Equipment						25						
Other	8	1	1	1	1	1	11	11	1	1	6	1
Bank credit line repaid								15	23	27	3	
Bank loan repaid							1	1	1	1	1	1
Total disbursements	191	174	172	172	174	238	223	235	220	220	198	180
Cash balance ending	18	9	8	8	8	8	8	8	8	8	10	10
Cumulative credit line			16	28	32	65	68	53	30	3		

Pro Forma Income Statement
September 30, 19X6
($ in 000s)

Sales	$2,300
Cost of goods sold	1,425
Gross profit	875
Operating expenses	800
Operating profit	75
Other expenses	20
Before-tax profit	55
Income taxes	12
Net profit	$ 43

Pro Forma Balance Sheet
September 30, 19X6
($ in 000s)

Cash	$ 15
Accounts receivable	199
Inventory	375
Prepaid expenses	55
Total current assets	644
Equipment (net)	155
Other assets	32
TOTAL ASSETS	$831
Notes payable	$ 84
Accounts payable	306
Other current liabilities	18
Total current liabilities	408
Long-term debt	140
TOTAL LIABILITIES	$548
NET WORTH	$283
TOTAL LIABILITIES AND NET WORTH	$831

POSSIBLE COLLATERAL

1. The major asset purchased with the money from the credit line will be Fremont tires. The inventory acquired could represent a source of collateral.

2. The 19X6 Ford 1.5-ton truck being purchased could be used as collateral.

Personal Financial Statement
Henry Jay
9-30-X5

ASSETS	
Cash	$ 4,000
Money market fund	6,200
Mutual fund	7,442
Common stock (Henry's Tire & Service)	192,000
Residence	160,000
Autos	27,000
Boat	18,500
Cash value of life insurance	6,000
Personal property	20,000
TOTAL ASSETS	$441,142

LIABILITIES AND NET WORTH	
Bank cards	$ 4,000
Accounts payable	6,100
Boat loan	7,200
Auto loans	11,200
Mortgage on residence	105,000
TOTAL LIABILITIES	$133,500
NET WORTH	$307,642
TOTAL LIABILITIES AND NET WORTH	$441,142

APPENDIX B

Basic Lending Documents

Documents courtesy of CFI Bankers Service Group, Inc.

CERTIFICATE OF ASSUMED NAME

KNOW ALL MEN BY THESE PRESENT: That the undersigned, doing business at ________________________________ ________________________ in the County of ____________ ________________ and State of Washington, under an assumed name and style, do hereby certify that the designation, name and style in which said business is to be conducted is ______ ____

and do further certify that the following persons are all of the persons conducting or intending to conduct said business or having an interest therein, and their true and real names, together with their respective post office addresses, are as follows:

____

P.O. Address ____

____

P.O. Address ____

____

P.O. Address ____

____

P.O. Address ____

____

P.O. Address ____

____

IN WITNESS WHEREOF, we have hereunto set our hands this ____________ day of ________________________ ________________________, A.D. ______19______.

____

____

____

____

____

COMMERCIAL PROMISSORY NOTE

Single Advance

(simple interest)

FOR LENDER USE ONLY

Account Number	Loan Number	Disbursement Date	Due Date	Principal Amount	Call Code	Collateral Code	Officer Number	Officer's Initials

References above to any particular loan or item do not limit the applicability of this note

Borrower: ____________________ **Lender:** ____________________

Principal Amount $ ____________ **Date of Note:** ____________

Borrower promises to pay to Lender, or order, ______________________________ DOLLARS together with interest on the unpaid principal balance outstanding from time to time at the rate set out below. Interest will accrue on the outstanding unpaid principal balance for each day that any amount is outstanding and will continue to accrue until this note is paid in full.

☐ Fixed Rate Loan. The interest rate on this note will be at a fixed rate of __________ per cent per annum.

☐ Variable Rate Loan. The interest rate on this note is subject to change from time to time as the Reference Rate described below changes from time to time. The following provisions, numbered (1) through (5), apply only if this is a variable rate loan:

(1) Rate Changes. Interest rate changes will occur:
☐ Whenever the Reference Rate changes.
☐ ______________________________

(2) Reference Rate. The Reference Rate for purposes of this note is:
☐ Lender's prime rate as announced from time to time ("Prime Rate"),
☐ An independent index or rate known as ______________________________ ("Index Rate"),
☐ A base rate set by Lender ______________________________ ("Base Rate").

(3) Interest Rate. The interest rate to be applied to the unpaid principal amount of this note shall be a rate of ______ percentage points ☐ over ☐ under the Reference Rate indicated above. That Reference Rate currently is __________ per cent per annum and thus the current rate on this note is __________ per cent per annum.

(4) Interest Ranges. Notwithstanding the foregoing provisions, under no circumstances shall the interest rate on this note be less than __________ per cent per annum or more than __________ per cent per annum.

(5) Payment Changes. Whenever increases occur in the interest rate, Lender may, but need not, change Borrower's payments to ensure that loan will pay off by its original maturity date and that payments cover accruing interest.

Interest shall be calculated on this note on the basis of 365/365 unless one of the following boxes is marked:
☐ 365/360 ☐ 30/360.

Borrower will pay this note as follows:

☐ Upon demand, or if no demand is made, then Borrower will pay this note on the following date or under the following schedule: ______________________________

☐ Borrower will pay this note on the following date or under the following schedule: ______________________________

☐ In addition to the payment(s) described above, Borrower will pay interest payments ☐ Monthly ☐ Quarterly ☐ At Maturity ☐ __________ beginning __________ and continuing each period thereafter until this note is paid in full.

Additional Provisions: ______________________________

If Borrower does not pay as agreed, or if Borrower or any guarantor of this note breaches any other agreement with Lender, Borrower will be in default. Upon default, or if Lender reasonably deems itself insecure, Lender may declare the entire unpaid principal balance and accrued interest immediately due, without notice, and Borrower will then pay that amount. Upon default Lender also may increase the interest rate at its option either __________ percentage points or to __________ per cent per annum and include any unpaid interest as of acceleration or maturity as part of the sum due and subject to the higher rate. The interest rate shall not exceed the maximum rate permitted by applicable law.

Borrower's payment will be late if not received within __________ days of the due date. If a payment is late, Borrower will be charged __________ % of the payment or $ __________ whichever is ☐ greater or ☐ less. Borrower will pay Lender at the address named above, or such other place as Lender may designate in writing.

Lender may pay someone else to help collect this note if Borrower does not pay. Borrower also will pay Lender that amount. This includes Lender's attorneys' fees whether or not there is a lawsuit, including attorneys' fees for bankruptcy proceedings, appeals, and anticipated post-judgment collection services. Borrower also will pay any court costs. Lender may delay enforcing any of its rights under this note without losing them. If there is a lawsuit, Borrower agrees to submit to the jurisdiction of the court in the county in which Lender is located.

Borrower waives presentment, demand for payment, protest, notice of dishonor, and notice of every other kind. The obligations of Borrower under this note are joint and several. The terms on the reverse side of this form are a part of this note.

____

By______________________________

By______________________________

ADDITIONAL TERMS ARE ON REVERSE

[reverse side]

These additional terms are a part of the terms of the note on the reverse side of this form.

Right of Set-Off.
Borrower authorizes Lender, to the extent permitted by applicable law, (a) upon default of any of its obligations to Lender, (b) at any time Lender reasonably deems itself insecure, or (c) in case of Borrower's death or insolvency, to charge or set off all sums owing on this note against any of Borrower's accounts with Lender (whether checking, savings, or some other account), including all accounts held jointly with someone else and all accounts Borrower may open in the future. Borrower grants Lender a contractual possessory security interest in Borrower's accounts to secure this right.

Reference Rates.
If the Variable Rate Loan box is marked on the reverse side, the interest rate on this loan may change from time to time as the Reference Rate indicated on the reverse side of this form changes in response to market forces that affect interest rates. That Reference Rate is not necessarily the lowest rate charged by Lender on its loans. Rather, it is an index used by Lender to set the rates on all loans made by Lender subject to the Reference Rate. Lender may make loans based on other rates as well. Borrower in executing this note agrees that Lender may set the loan rate based upon the Reference Rate.

The Prime Rate shown on the reverse side, if marked as the Reference Rate for this loan, is a traditional prime rate. This is the rate Lender charges, or would charge, on ninety-day unsecured loans to the most credit worthy corporate customers. This may not be the lowest rate available from Lender at any given time.

The Index Rate shown on the reverse side, if marked as the Reference Rate for this loan, is an independent index (such as another lender's prime lending rate) over which Lender has no control. If the index becomes unavailable during the term of this loan, Lender may designate a substitute index.

The Base Rate shown on the reverse side, if marked as the Reference Rate for this loan, is set by Lender in its sole discretion. Lender may subsequently designate an independent index as the Lender Rate, but will notify Borrower before doing so.

The Reference Rate in effect at any time on this note is available from Lender.

Miscellaneous Provisions.
Unless the parties agree otherwise, payments will be applied first to any collection costs, then to any late charges, then to accrued unpaid interest, and any remaining amount to principal.

If the Lender does not increase the rate of interest on this note in the event of a breach or other default, then the interest rate will continue at the stated note rate.

NO. DUE NAME

DATE	INTEREST		PAID TO	PRIN. PMT.		BALANCE	

FOR LENDER USE ONLY

Account Number	Loan Number	Date of Note	Due Date	Principal Amount

References above to any particular loan or item do not limit the applicability of this agreement

PARTNERSHIP BORROWING AGREEMENT

Partnership:

Lender:

The names and addresses of all Partners (limited partners, if any, should be specified as such) in the Partnership are:

Names	**Mailing Addresses**

The Designated Partners are:

In consideration of the existing or proposed lending or banking relationship between the Partnership and Lender, the persons signing below jointly and severally represent to Lender and agree with Lender that:

1. We are all of the general partners of the Partnership. We also have listed above all of the limited partners, if any, in the Partnership. We agree to notify Lender of any change in the Partnership, including the adding of new partners and the leaving of current partners from the Partnership, before the change takes effect.
2. The partnership name filled in above is the complete and correct name of the Partnership. The following is a complete list of all assumed business names, if any, under which the Partnership does business:

   The Partnership has filed assumed business name listings with the following governmental entities on the indicated dates:

3. Any of the Designated Partners listed above may enter into any agreements of any nature with Lender, and those agreements will bind the Partnership. In addition, each of the Partners listed above will be jointly and severally liable for the obligations of the Partnership; however, any limited partners listed above and identified as such will not be liable individually beyond their interest in the Partnership plus any liability created under applicable law or under any other agreements with Lender (such as a guaranty).

   Without limiting the kinds of agreements covered by this provision, any Designated Partner may borrow money in the Partnership name, give security, guarantee obligations, and sign any documents relating to such agreements (such as notes, mortgages, deeds of trust, security agreements, assignments, guaranties, and collateral agreements).
4. We will notify Lender, in writing, prior to any change in the name of the Partnership, in the assumed business names of the Partnership, in the Designated Partners, or in any other aspect of the Partnership that directly or indirectly relates to any agreements between the Partnership and Lender. No change in the name of the Partnership will take effect until after Lender has been so notified.

The rights of Lender under this agreement are in addition to any other rights Lender may have. Lender need not accept this agreement for it to become effective. This agreement is dated: ______________________.

(Signatures of all general partners)

FOR LENDER USE ONLY

Account Number	Loan Number	Date of Note	Due Date	Principal Amount

References above to a particular loan do not limit the applicability of this Resolution

CORPORATE RESOLUTION TO BORROW OR GUARANTEE

Lender: ______

Corporation: ______

I, the undersigned Secretary of the Corporation named above, hereby certify as follows: The Corporation is organized and existing under and by virtue of the laws of the State of: ______. The Corporation has its principal office at: ______. The officers of the Corporation are as follows:

Name	Position

I further certify that at a meeting of the Directors of the Corporation, duly and regularly called and held on the ______ day of ______, 19 ______, at which a quorum was present and voting, the following resolutions were unanimously adopted:

BE IT RESOLVED, that any ______ of the following named officers or employees of this Corporation, whose actual signatures are shown below:

Name (please type)	Position	Actual Signature

acting for and on behalf of this Corporation and as its act and deed, be and they are hereby authorized and empowered:

(a) To borrow from Lender, on such terms as may be agreed upon between the officers or employees and Lender, such sum or sums of money as in their judgment should be borrowed, not exceeding, however, at any one time the aggregate amount of ☐ Unlimited ☐ ______ ($ ______).

(b) To guarantee or act as surety for loan(s) to ______, from Lender on such terms as may be agreed upon between the officers or employees and Lender, such sum or sums of money as in their judgment should be guaranteed or assured, not exceeding, however, at any one time the aggregate amount of ☐ Unlimited ☐ ______ ($ ______).

(c) To execute and deliver to Lender the promissory note or notes of the Corporation, on Lender's forms, at such rates of interest and on such terms as may be agreed upon, evidencing the sums of money so borrowed or any indebtedness of the Corporation to Lender, and also to execute and deliver to Lender any renewal or renewals of the notes, or any of them, or of any part thereof.

(d) To mortgage, pledge, hypothecate, or otherwise encumber and deliver to Lender, as security for the payment of any loans so obtained, any promissory notes so executed, or any other or further indebtedness of the Corporation to Lender at any time owing, however the same may be evidenced, any property belonging to the Corporation or in which the Corporation may have an interest, real, personal or mixed. Such property may be encumbered, hypothecated, or pledged at the time such loans are obtained or such indebtedness is incurred, or at any other time or times, and may be either in addition to or in lieu of any property theretofore mortgaged, hypothecated, encumbered, or pledged. The provisions of these Resolutions authorizing or relating to the pledge, hypothecation, granting of a security interest in, or otherwise in any way encumbrancing the assets of the Corporation shall include, without limitation, doing so in order to lend collateral support to indebtedness, now existing or later arising and of any nature whatsoever, of ______ to Lender. The Corporation has considered the value to itself of lending collateral in support of such indebtedness, and the Corporation represents to Lender that the Corporation is benefited by doing so.

(e) To execute and deliver to Lender the form of pledge agreement, security agreement, and financing statement which may be submitted by Lender, and which shall evidence the terms and conditions under and pursuant to which such pledges, or any of them, are made; and also to execute and deliver to Lender any mortgages, deeds, trust indentures, or other instruments in writing, of any kind or nature, which may be necessary or proper in connection therewith or pertaining thereto.

(f) To draw, endorse, and discount with Lender drafts, trade acceptances, promissory notes, or other evidences of indebtedness payable or belonging to the Corporation or in which the Corporation may have an interest, and either to receive cash for the same or to cause such proceeds to be credited to the account of the Corporation with Lender, or to cause such other disposition of the proceeds derived therefrom as they may deem advisable.

(g) To do and perform such other acts and things and to execute and deliver such other documents as may in their discretion be deemed reasonably necessary or proper in order to carry into effect any of the provisions of these Resolutions.

BE IT FURTHER RESOLVED, that these Resolutions shall remain in full force and effect until written notice of the revocation thereof shall have been delivered to and received by Lender. Any such notice shall not affect any agreements in effect or committed at the time notice is given.

I further certify that the persons hereinabove named occupy the positions set opposite their respective names; that the foregoing Resolutions now stand of record on the books of the Corporation; that they are in full force and effect and have not been modified or revoked in any manner whatsoever.

IN TESTIMONY WHEREOF, I have hereunto set my hand and affixed the seal of the Corporation this ______ day of ______, 19 ______.

CORPORATE SEAL

Secretary ______

*Director ______

Title ______ (See footnote)

*NOTE: In case the Secretary or other certifying officer is designated by the foregoing resolutions as one of the signing officers, this certificate must also be signed by a second Officer or Director of the Corporation.

FOR LENDER USE ONLY	Account Number	Loan Number	Date of Note	Due Date	Principal Amount

References above to a particular loan or item do not limit the applicability of this Guaranty.

COMMERCIAL GUARANTY

Borrower: ______________________ Lender: ______________________

Guarantor: ______________________

The Principal Amount of this Guaranty is ______________________ Dollars ($______________).

For valuable consideration Guarantor jointly and severally and unconditionally guarantees and promises to pay to Lender, its successors or assigns, on demand in lawful money of the United States of America, any and all Indebtedness of Borrower to Lender, as follows:

1. **"Indebtedness" Defined.** The word "Indebtedness" is used in this Guaranty in its most comprehensive sense and includes, but is not limited to, any and all advances, debts, obligations, and liabilities of Borrower, or any of them, including judgments against Borrower, heretofore, now, or hereafter made, incurred, or created, whether voluntarily or involuntarily and however arising, whether due or not due, absolute or contingent, liquidated or unliquidated, determined or undetermined, and whether Borrower may be liable individually or jointly with others, or primarily or secondarily, or as guarantor, and whether recovery upon such indebtedness may be or hereafter may become barred by any statute of limitations, and whether such indebtedness may be or hereafter may become otherwise unenforceable, and whether such indebtedness arises from transactions which may be voidable on account of infancy, insanity, ultra vires, or otherwise.

2. **Maximum Liability.** The liability of Guarantor under this Guaranty shall not exceed at any one time the sum of the Principal Amount set forth above, plus all interest thereon and plus all of Lender's costs, expenses, and attorney fees, including any on appeals, in connection with the enforcement of this Guaranty, the collection of the Indebtedness of Borrower, or with the collection or sale of any collateral, whether or not there is a lawsuit.

   The above limitation on liability is not a restriction on the amount of the Indebtedness of Borrower to Lender either in the aggregate or at any one time. If Lender presently holds one or more guaranties or hereafter receives additional guaranties from Guarantor of the Indebtedness of Borrower, the rights of Lender under all guaranties shall be cumulative. This Guaranty shall not, unless herein provided, affect or invalidate any such other guaranties. The liability of Guarantor will be the aggregate liability of Guarantor under the terms of this Guaranty and any such other unterminated guaranties.

3. **Nature of Guaranty.** The liability of Guarantor shall be open and continuous for so long as this Guaranty is in force. Guarantor intends to guarantee at all times the performance of all obligations of Borrower to Lender within the limits of Section 2. Thus, no payments made upon Borrower's Indebtedness will discharge or diminish the liability of Guarantor for any and all remaining and succeeding Indebtedness of Borrower to Lender. The liability of Guarantor will be enforceable against both the separate and community property of Guarantor whether now owned or hereafter acquired.

4. **Duration of Guaranty.** This Guaranty will take effect when received by Lender, without the necessity of any acceptance by Lender, and will continue in full force until such time as Guarantor notifies Lender in writing of Guarantor's election to revoke this Guaranty. Guarantor's written notice of revocation must be delivered to Lender at the branch or office of Lender as listed above. Written revocation of this Guaranty shall apply only to advances or new Indebtedness created after actual receipt by Lender of Guarantor's written revocation. This Guaranty will continue to bind Guarantor for all Indebtedness incurred by Borrower or committed by Lender prior to receipt of Guarantor's written notice of revocation including any extension, renewal, or modification thereof. Renewals, extensions, and modifications of Borrower's Indebtedness, granted after Guarantor's revocation, are contemplated hereunder and will specifically not be considered new Indebtedness. This Guaranty shall bind the estate of Guarantor as to Indebtedness created both before and after the death or incapacity of Guarantor, regardless of Lender's actual notice of Guarantor's death or incapacity, provided, that Guarantor's executor or administrator, or other legal representative may terminate this Guaranty in the same manner in which Guarantor might have terminated it and with the same effect. Termination of this Guaranty by one of the undersigned shall not affect the liability hereunder of the remaining of the undersigned.

   It is anticipated that fluctuations may occur in the aggregate amount of Indebtedness covered by this Guaranty and it is specifically acknowledged and agreed by Guarantor that reductions in the amount of Indebtedness, even to zero (0) dollars, prior to written revocation of this Guaranty by Guarantor shall not constitute a termination of this Guaranty.

5. **Guarantor's Authorization to Lender.** Guarantor authorizes Lender, either before or after revocation hereof, without notice or demand and without affecting Guarantor's liability hereunder, from time to time to (a) make additional secured or unsecured loans to Borrower; (b) alter, compromise, renew, extend, accelerate, or otherwise change the time for payment of, or otherwise change the terms of the Indebtedness or any part thereof, including an increase or decrease of the rate of interest thereon; (c) take and hold security for the payment of this Guaranty or the Indebtedness guaranteed, and exchange, enforce, waive, and release any such security, with or without the substitution of new collateral; (d) release, substitute, agree not to sue, or deal with any one or more of Borrower's sureties, endorsers, or other guarantors (including Guarantors under this Guaranty) on any terms or manner Lender chooses; (e) apply such security and direct the order or manner of sale thereof, including, without limitation, a nonjudicial sale permitted by the terms of the controlling security agreement or deed of trust, as Lender in its discretion may determine; and (f) assign this Guaranty in whole or in part without notice.

6. **Guarantor's Warranties.** Guarantor warrants that: (a) this Guaranty is executed at Borrower's request and not at the request of the Lender; (b) Guarantor has not and will not, without prior written consent of Lender, sell, lease, assign, encumber, hypothecate, transfer, or otherwise dispose of all or substantially all of Guarantor's assets, or any interest therein; (c) Guarantor has established adequate means of obtaining from Borrower on a continuing basis information regarding Borrower's financial condition; and (d) Lender has made no representation to Guarantor as to the creditworthiness of Borrower. Guarantor agrees to keep adequately informed from such means of any facts, events, or circumstances which might in any way affect Guarantor's risks hereunder, and Guarantor further agrees that absent a request for information Lender shall have no obligation to disclose to Guarantor information or material acquired in the course of Lender's relationship with Borrower.

[reverse side]

7. **Guarantor's Waivers.** Guarantor waives any right to require Lender to (a) make any presentment, protest, demand, or notice of any kind, including notice of any nonpayment of Borrower's Indebtedness or of any collateral thereto and notice of any action or nonaction on the part of Borrower, Lender, any surety, endorser, or other guarantor (including any Guarantor under this Guaranty) in connection with the Indebtedness guaranteed hereunder, or in connection with the creation of new or additional Indebtedness; (b) proceed directly or at once against any person, including Borrower; (c) proceed directly against or exhaust any collateral held from Borrower, any other guarantor (including any Guarantor under this Guaranty), or any other person; (d) give notice of the terms, time, and place of any public or private sale of personal property security held from Borrower or comply with any other applicable provisions of the Uniform Commercial Code; or (e) pursue any other remedy in Lender's power.

   Guarantor waives any rights or defenses arising by reason of (a) any law which may prevent Lender from bringing any action, including a claim for deficiency, against Guarantor, before or after Lender's commencement or completion of any foreclosure action, either judicial or by exercise of a power of sale; (b) any election of remedies by Lender which destroys Guarantor's subrogation rights or Guarantor's rights to proceed against Borrower for reimbursement, including without limitation any loss of rights Guarantor may suffer by reason of any law limiting, qualifying, or discharging Borrower's Indebtedness; (c) any disability or other defense of Borrower, any other guarantor (including any Guarantor under this Guaranty), any other person, or by reason of the cessation from any cause whatsoever other than payment in full of the Indebtedness of Borrower; (d) any statute of limitations, if at any time any action or suit brought by Lender against Guarantor is commenced there is outstanding an Indebtedness of Borrower to Lender which is not banned by any applicable statute of limitations. If payment is made by Borrower on Indebtedness guaranteed hereby and thereafter Lender is forced to remit the amount of that payment to Borrower's trustee in bankruptcy or similar person under any federal or state bankruptcy law or law for the relief of debtors, Borrower's Indebtedness shall be considered unpaid for the purpose of enforcement of this Guaranty.

8. **Guarantor's Understanding With Respect to Waivers.** Guarantor warrants and agrees that each of the waivers set forth above is made with Guarantor's full knowledge of its significance and consequences, and that under the circumstances, the waivers are reasonable and not contrary to public policy or law. If any of such waivers is determined to be contrary to any applicable law or public policy, such waiver shall be effective only to the extent permitted by law.

9. **Lender's Rights With Respect to Guarantor's Property in Possession of Lender.** In addition to all liens upon, and rights of setoff against the moneys, securities, or other property of Guarantor given to Lender by law, Lender shall have a security interest in and a right of setoff against all moneys, securities, and other property of Guarantor now or hereafter in the possession of or on deposit with Lender, whether held in a general or special account or deposit, or for safekeeping or otherwise. Every such security interest and right of setoff may be exercised without demand upon or notice to Guarantor. No security interest or right of setoff shall be deemed to have been waived by any act or conduct on the part of Lender, or by any neglect to exercise such right of setoff or to enforce such security interest, or by any delay in so doing. Every right of setoff and security interest shall continue in full force and effect until such right of setoff or security interest is specifically waived or released by an instrument in writing executed by Lender.

10. **Subordination of Borrower's Debts to Guarantor.** Guarantor agrees that the Indebtedness of Borrower to Lender, whether now existing or hereafter created, shall be prior to any claim that Guarantor may now have or hereafter acquire against Borrower, whether or not Borrower becomes insolvent. Guarantor hereby expressly subordinates any claim Guarantor may have against Borrower, upon any account whatsoever, to any claim that Lender may now or hereafter have against Borrower. In the event of insolvency and consequent liquidation of the assets of Borrower, through bankruptcy, by an assignment for the benefit of creditors, by voluntary liquidation, or otherwise, the assets of Borrower applicable to the payment of the claims of both Lender and Guarantor shall be paid to Lender and shall be first applied by Lender to the Indebtedness of Borrower to Lender. Guarantor does hereby assign to Lender all claims which it may have or acquire against Borrower or any assignee or trustee in bankruptcy of Borrower; provided, that such assignment shall be effective only for the purpose of assuring to Lender full payment of all Indebtedness of Borrower to Lender. Any notes now or hereafter evidencing such Indebtedness of Borrower to Guarantor shall be marked with a legend that the same are subject to this Guaranty and, if Lender so requests, shall be delivered to Lender. Guarantor will, and Lender is hereby authorized, in the name of Guarantor from time to time to execute and file financing statements and continuation statements and execute such other documents and take such other action as Lender deems necessary or appropriate to perfect, preserve, and enforce its rights hereunder.

11. **Waiver of Authentication of Validity of Acts of Corporation or Partnership.** If any one or more of Borrower or Guarantor are corporations or partnerships, it is not necessary for Lender to inquire into the powers of Borrower or Guarantor or the officers, directors, partners, or agents acting or purporting to act on their behalf, and any Indebtedness made or created in reliance upon the professed exercise of such powers shall be guaranteed hereunder.

12. **Obligations of Married Persons.** Any married person who signs this Guaranty as the Guarantor hereby expressly agrees that recourse may be had against his or her separate property for all his or her obligations under this Guaranty.

13. **Application of Singular and Plural in Context and Construction.** In all cases where there are more than one Borrower or Guarantor, then all words used herein in the singular shall be deemed to have been used in the plural where the context and construction so require; and where there is more than one Borrower named herein, or when this Guaranty is executed by more than one Guarantor, the word "Borrower" and the word "Guarantor" respectively shall mean all and any one or more of them.

14. **Applicable Laws.** This Guaranty is governed by and construed in accordance with the laws of the state where Lender's office is located as shown on the reverse side of this Guaranty.

THIS GUARANTY IS EFFECTIVE UNTIL TERMINATED IN THE MANNER SET FORTH IN PARAGRAPH 4.

The undersigned Guarantor has executed this Guaranty on ______________________
(Date)

____
Guarantor

____
Guarantor

[page 1]

FOR LENDER USE ONLY	Account Number	Loan Number	Date of Note	Due Date	Principal Amount	COMMERCIAL SECURITY AGREEMENT
	References above to a particular loan or item do not limit the applicability of this Security Agreement.					

Borrower: ______________________ **Lender:** ______________________

Location of Collateral (if different from Borrower's address): ______________________

Grant of Security Interest. For value received, and to secure both the payment of the Indebtedness owed to Lender and the performance of the obligations under this Security Agreement and any Related Documents, and in accordance with the definitions and terms set forth below, Borrower grants Lender a security interest in all of the following Collateral:

☐ All of the Collateral described in Schedule(s) / Addenda covering ______________, attached to this Security Agreement and incorporated by reference in this Security Agreement.
☐ All Inventory (including Dealer Inventory)
☐ All Chattel Paper
☐ All Accounts and Contract Rights
☐ All Equipment
☐ All General Intangibles
☐ All Crops
☐ All Fixtures
☐ All Farm Equipment and Farm Products (including Livestock)
☐ ______________________

Borrower agrees to insure the Collateral for at least $ ____________, on a (check which applies) ☐ replacement value ☐ cash value.

1. **Definitions.**

1.1 **Indebtedness.** "Indebtedness" shall mean all amounts and liabilities of every kind and description, whether now owed or hereafter owed by Borrower to Lender, whether or not evidenced by a promissory note or credit agreement and whether direct, indirect, or contingent.

1.2 **Related Documents.** "Related Documents" shall mean the promissory notes, loan agreements, guaranties, trust deeds, mortgages, other security agreements, or any other documents executed in connection with this Security Agreement or the Indebtedness, whether already existing or executed now or later.

1.3 **Additional Grantor.** Any "Additional Grantor" who cosigns this Security Agreement but does not execute the promissory note or other debt instrument is cosigning this Security Agreement only to grant Lender a security interest in the Collateral under this Security Agreement to secure the Indebtedness, and is not personally liable on the note or debt instrument except as otherwise provided by law or contract. Additional Grantor agrees that Lender and Borrower may agree to extend, modify, forebear, or make any other accommodations or amendments with regard to the Indebtedness or this Security Agreement without Additional Grantor's consent and without releasing Additional Grantor or modifying this Security Agreement as to Additional Grantor's interest in the Collateral. Additional Grantor acknowledges that Lender is relying on its participation in this Security Agreement and would not extend or maintain the Indebtedness otherwise. References to "Borrower" include the Additional Grantor except to the extent any such reference creates liability on the Indebtedness beyond the Collateral. The Additional Grantor's name and address are:

____

1.4 **Collateral.** "Collateral" shall mean the collateral described above, whether now owned or hereafter acquired, whether now existing or hereafter arising, and wherever located; and

(a) All accessions, parts, or additions to and all replacements of and substitutions for any of the property described above; and

(b) All proceeds (including insurance proceeds) from the sale or other disposition of any of the property described above, including that described in the preceding subparagraph.

(c) In addition to all liens upon, and rights of setoff against the moneys, securities, or other property of Borrower given to Lender by law, Lender shall have a security interest in and a right of setoff against all moneys, securities, and other property of Borrower now or hereafter in the possession of or on deposit with Lender, whether held in a general or special account or deposit, or for safekeeping or otherwise; and every such security interest and right of setoff may be exercised without demand upon or notice to Borrower. No security interest or right of setoff shall be deemed to have been waived by any act or conduct on the part of Lender, or by any neglect to exercise such right of setoff or to enforce such security interest, or by any delay in so doing; and every right of setoff and security interest shall continue in full force and effect until such right of setoff or security interest is specifically waived or released by an instrument in writing executed by Lender.

[page 2]

2. **Obligations of Borrower.**

Borrower warrants and covenants:

2.1 **Perfection of Security Interest.** Borrower agrees to execute financing statements and to take whatever other action is requested by Lender to perfect and continue Lender's security interest in the Collateral. Upon request of Lender, Borrower will deliver to Lender any and all documents evidencing or constituting the Collateral, and Borrower will note Lender's interest upon any and all chattel paper. Borrower hereby appoints Lender the Borrower's irrevocable attorney in fact for the purpose of executing any documents necessary to perfect or to continue the security interest granted herein. Lender may at any time, and without further authorization from Borrower, file copies of this Security Agreement as a financing statement. Borrower will reimburse Lender for all expenses for perfecting or continuing this security interest.

2.2 **Removal of Collateral.** Borrower warrants that the Collateral (or to the extent the Collateral consists of intangible property such as accounts, the records concerning the Collateral) is located at Borrower's address or the Collateral address shown above.

Except in the ordinary course of its business within the county in which the Collateral is located, Borrower shall not remove the Collateral from its location without the prior written consent of Lender, which shall not be unreasonably withheld. To the extent the Collateral constitutes vehicles, or other titled property, and except for sales of inventory in the ordinary course of its business, Borrower shall not take or permit any action which would require registration of the vehicles outside of the state in which the Lender is located, without the prior written consent of Lender.

2.3 **Transactions Involving Collateral.** Except for inventory sold or accounts collected in the ordinary course of Borrower's business, Borrower shall not sell, offer to sell, or otherwise transfer the Collateral. Borrower shall not pledge mortgage, encumber or otherwise permit the Collateral to be subject to any lien, security interest, or charge, other than the security interest provided for herein, without the prior written consent of Lender. This includes security interests even if junior in right to this Security Agreement. Unless waived by Lender, all proceeds from any disposition of the Collateral (for whatever reason) shall be held in trust for Lender, and shall not be commingled with any other funds; provided, however, that this requirement shall not constitute consent by Lender to any sale or other disposition. Borrower shall immediately deliver any such proceeds to Lender.

2.4 **Title.** Borrower warrants that it holds marketable title to the Collateral subject only to the lien of this Security Agreement. Borrower shall defend Lender's rights against the claims and demands of all persons.

2.5 **Use.** Borrower shall keep the Collateral in first class condition and repair. Borrower will not commit or permit damage to or destruction of the Collateral or any part thereof.

2.6 **Taxes, Assessments and Liens.** Borrower will pay when due all taxes, assessments, and liens upon the Collateral, its use or operation, upon this Security Agreement, upon any promissory notes evidencing the Indebtedness or upon any of the other Related Documents. Borrower may withhold any such payment or may elect to contest any lien if Borrower is in good faith conducting appropriate proceedings to contest the obligation to pay and so long as Lender's interest in the Collateral is not jeopardized. If the Collateral is subjected to a lien which is not discharged within 15 days, Borrower shall deposit with Lender cash, a sufficient corporate surety bond or other security satisfactory to Lender in an amount adequate to provide for the discharge of the lien plus any interest, costs, attorneys' fees or other charges that could accrue as a result of foreclosure or sale. In any contest Borrower shall defend itself and Lender and shall satisfy any final adverse judgment before enforcement against the Collateral. Borrower shall name Lender as an additional obligee under any surety bond furnished in the contest proceedings.

2.7 **Compliance With Governmental Requirements.** Borrower shall comply promptly with all laws, ordinances and regulations of all governmental authorities applicable to the use of the Collateral. Borrower may contest in good faith any such law, ordinance or regulation and withhold compliance during any proceeding, including appropriate appeals, so long as Lender's interest in the Collateral is not jeopardized.

2.8 **Maintenance of Casualty Insurance.** Borrower shall procure and maintain policies of fire and other casualty insurance with standard extended coverage covering the Collateral on the basis and in at least the amount described above, and with loss payable to Lender. Policies shall be written by insurance companies reasonably acceptable to Lender. Borrower shall deliver to Lender certificates of coverage from each insurer containing a stipulation that coverage will not be cancelled or diminished without a minimum of 10 days prior written notice to Lender.

2.9 **Application of Insurance Proceeds.** Borrower shall promptly notify Lender of any loss or damage to the Collateral or any portion thereof having a fair market value in excess of $1,000. Lender may make proof of loss if Borrower fails to do so within 15 days of the casualty. All proceeds of any insurance on the Collateral shall be held by Lender as part of the Collateral. If Borrower and Lender agree to repair or replace the damaged or destroyed Collateral, Lender shall, upon satisfactory proof of expenditure, pay or reimburse Borrower from the proceeds for the reasonable cost of repair or restoration. If Borrower and Lender do not agree to restore the Collateral, Lender shall retain a sufficient amount of the proceeds to pay all of the Indebtedness, and shall pay the balance to Borrower. Any proceeds which have not been paid out within 180 days after their receipt and which Borrower has not committed to the repair or restoration of the Collateral shall be used to prepay the Indebtedness.

2.10 **Insurance Reserves.** Lender may require Borrower to maintain with Lender reserves for payment of insurance premiums which reserves shall be created by monthly payments of a sum estimated by Lender to be sufficient to produce, at least 15 days before due, amounts at least equal to the insurance premiums to be paid. If 15 days before payment is due the reserve funds are insufficient, Borrower shall upon demand pay any deficiency to Lender. The reserve funds shall be held by Lender as a general deposit from Borrower and shall constitute a noninterest-bearing debt from Lender to Borrower which Lender may satisfy by payment of the insurance premiums required to be paid by Borrower as they become due. Lender does not hold the reserve funds in trust for Borrower, and Lender is not the agent of Borrower for payment of the insurance premiums required to be paid by Borrower.

[page 3]

2.11 **Borrower's Report On Insurance.** If requested by Lender within 60 days after the close of Borrower's fiscal year, Borrower shall furnish to Lender a report on each existing policy of insurance showing:

(a) the name of the insurer;
(b) the risks insured;
(c) the amount of the policy;
(d) the property insured;
(e) the then current value on the basis of which insurance has been obtained, and the manner of determining that value; and
(f) the expiration date of the policy.

Borrower shall upon request have an independent appraiser satisfactory to Lender determine, as applicable, the cash value or replacement cost of the Collateral.

3. **Borrower's Right to Possession.**

Until default, Borrower may have possession of the tangible personal property and beneficial use of all of the Collateral and may use it in any lawful manner not inconsistent with this Security Agreement or the Related Documents.

4. **Expenditures by Lender.**

If not discharged or paid by Borrower when due, Lender may discharge taxes, liens, security interests, or other encumbrances at any time levied or placed on the Collateral, may pay for insurance on the Collateral, and may pay for maintenance and preservation of the Collateral. All such payments shall become a part of Borrower's obligations secured hereby, payable on demand, with interest at the maximum rate permitted by law from date of expenditure until repaid. Such right shall be in addition to any other rights or remedies to which Lender may be entitled on account of default.

5. **Events of Default.**

Borrower shall be in default under this Security Agreement upon:

(a) Failure to make any payment of the Indebtedness when due; or
(b) Failure to comply within 15 days after written notice from Lender demanding compliance with any other term, obligation, covenant or condition contained herein (or in any of the Related Documents); provided, if compliance is not possible within 15 days, default shall occur upon failure within 15 days to take steps that will produce compliance as soon as is reasonably practical; or
(c) Any warranty, representation, or statement made or furnished to Lender by or on behalf of Borrower proves to have been false in any material respect when made or furnished; or
(d) Borrower's death (if Borrower is an individual), dissolution or termination of Borrower's existence as a going business, insolvency, appointment of a receiver for any part of Borrower's property, any assignment for the benefit of creditors, or the commencement of any proceeding under any bankruptcy or insolvency laws by or against Borrower; or
(e) Commencement of foreclosure, whether by judicial proceeding, self-help, repossession, or any other method, by any creditor of Borrower against any of the Collateral, but this subsection shall not apply in the event of a good faith dispute by Borrower as to the validity or reasonableness of the claim which is the basis of the foreclosure suit, provided that Borrower provides Lender with written notice of such claim and provides adequate reserves therefor.

6. **Rights of Lender.**

6.1 **Rights Prior To Default or Thereafter.** Lender and its designated representatives or agents may at all reasonable times examine and inspect the Collateral, wherever located.

6.2 **Rights Upon Default or Thereafter.** Upon default, or if Lender reasonably deems itself insecure, Lender may exercise any one or more of the following rights and remedies in addition to any other rights or remedies that may be available at law, in equity, or otherwise:

(a) Lender may declare the entire Indebtedness including any prepayment penalty which Borrower would be required to pay, immediately due and payable.
(b) Lender may require Borrower to deliver to Lender all or any portion of the Collateral and any and all certificates of title and other documents relating thereto. Lender may require Borrower to assemble the Collateral and make it available to Lender at a place to be designated by Lender which is reasonably convenient to both parties. Lender also shall have full power to enter upon the property of Borrower to take possession of and remove the Collateral.
(c) Lender shall have full power to sell, lease, transfer, or otherwise deal with the Collateral or proceeds thereof in its own name or that of Borrower. Lender may sell the Collateral at public auction. Unless the Collateral threatens to decline speedily in value or is of the type customarily sold on a recognized market, Lender will give Borrower reasonable notice of the time after which any private sale or any other intended disposition thereof is to be made. The requirements of reasonable notice shall be met if such notice is mailed by registered or certified mail, postage prepaid, to the address of Borrower stated in this Security Agreement at least 10 days before the time of the sale or disposition. Borrower shall be liable for expenses of retaking, holding, preparing for sale, selling, and the like.
(d) Lender may have a receiver appointed as a matter of right. The receiver may be an employee of Lender and may serve without bond. All fees of the receiver and his attorney shall be secured hereby.
(e) Lender may revoke Borrower's right to collect the rents and revenues from the Collateral, and may, either itself or through a receiver, collect the same. To facilitate collection, Lender may notify any account debtors of Borrower to pay directly to Lender.
(f) Lender may obtain a judgment for any deficiency remaining in the Indebtedness due to Lender after application of all amounts received from the exercise of the rights provided in this section. Borrower shall be liable for a deficiency even if the underlying transaction is a sale of accounts or chattel paper.
(g) Lender shall have and may exercise any or all of the rights and remedies of a secured creditor under the provisions of the Uniform Commercial Code, at law, in equity, or otherwise.

[page 4]

7. **Waiver.**

Lender shall not be deemed to have waived any rights hereunder (or under the Related Documents) unless such waiver be in writing and signed by Lender. No delay or omission on the part of Lender in exercising any right shall operate as a waiver of such right or any other right. A waiver by any party of a breach of a provision of this Security Agreement shall not constitute a waiver of or prejudice the party's right otherwise to demand strict compliance with that provision or any other provision. Whenever consent by Lender is required herein, the granting of such consent by Lender in any instance shall not constitute continuing consent to subsequent instances where such consent is required herein.

8. **Remedies Cumulative.**

All of the Lender's rights and remedies, whether evidenced hereby or by any other writing, shall be cumulative and may be exercised singularly or concurrently. Election by Lender to pursue any remedy shall not exclude pursuit of any other remedy, and an election to make expenditures or take action to perform an obligation of Borrower under this Security Agreement after Borrower's failure to perform shall not affect Lender's right to declare a default and exercise its remedies under Section 6.

9. **Successor Interests.**

This Security Agreement shall be binding upon and inure to the benefit of the parties, their successors, and assigns, but whenever there is no outstanding Indebtedness, Borrower may terminate this Security Agreement upon written notice to Lender.

10. **Notice.**

Any notice under this Security Agreement shall be in writing and shall be effective when actually delivered or when deposited in the mail, registered or certified, addressed to the parties at the addresses stated herein or such other addresses as either party may designate by written notice to the other.

11. **Expenses, Costs, and Attorneys' Fees.**

In the event Lender is required to commence any suit or action to enforce any of the terms of this Security Agreement, Lender shall be entitled to recover from Borrower reasonable attorneys' fees and legal expenses at trial and also such fees and expenses on appeal, in addition to all other sums provided by law. In the event that Lender is otherwise required to incur any expenses whatsoever to protect or enforce its rights hereunder, whether or not litigation is commenced, Lender shall be entitled to recover any and all such sums and all incidental expenses, including such reasonable attorneys' fees. All such sums shall be part of the Indebtedness secured hereby.

12. **Applicable Law.**

This Security Agreement is accepted in and shall be governed by the laws of the state in which the Lender is located.

13. **Multiple Parties; Corporate Authority.**

If Borrower consists of more than one person or entity, all obligations of Borrower under this Security Agreement shall be joint and several. Where any one or more of Borrowers are corporations or partnerships it is not necessary for Lender to inquire into the powers of Borrowers or the officers, directors, partners, or agents acting or purporting to act on their behalf, and any Indebtedness made or created in reliance upon the professed exercise of such powers shall be guaranteed hereunder.

14. **Special Provisions:**

IN WITNESS WHEREOF, the parties have executed this Security Agreement as of the dates shown below.

LENDER:

____

By ______________________________

Date ______________________________

BORROWER:

____

By ______________________________

By ______________________________

Date ______________________________

ADDITIONAL GRANTOR:

____

By ______________________________

By ______________________________

Date ______________________________

FINANCING STATEMENT

STANDARD FORM

JULIUS BLUMBERG, INC. N. Y. C. 10013

UNIFORM COMMERCIAL CODE – FINANCING STATEMENT – FORM UCC-1

INSTRUCTIONS

1. PLEASE TYPE this form. Fold only along perforation for mailing.
2. Remove Secured Party and Debtor copies and send other 3 copies with interleaved carbon paper to the filing officer. Enclose filing fee.
3. If the space provided for any item(s) on the form is inadequate the item(s) should be continued on additional sheets, preferably 5" x 8" or 8" x 10". Only one copy of such additional sheets need be presented to the filing officer with a set of three copies of the financing statement. Long schedules of collateral, indentures, etc., may be on any size paper that is convenient for the secured party. Indicate the number of additional sheets attached.
4. If collateral is crops or goods which are or are to become fixtures, describe generally the real estate and give name of record owner.
5. When a copy of the security agreement is used as a financing statement, it is requested that it be accompanied by a completed but unsigned set of these forms, without extra fee.
6. At the time of original filing, filing officer should return third copy as an acknowledgement. At a later time, secured party may date and sign Termination Legend and use third copy as a Termination Statement.

This **FINANCING STATEMENT** is presented to a filing officer for filing pursuant to the Uniform Commercial Code: | 3. Maturity date (if any):

1. Debtor(s) (Last Name First) and address(es)	2. Secured Party(ies) and address(es)	For Filing Officer (Date, Time, Number, and Filing Office)
4. This financing statement covers the following types (or items) of property:		5. Assignee(s) of Secured Party and Address(es)

This statement is filed without the debtor's signature to perfect a security interest in collateral. (check ☒ if so) | Filed with:

☐ already subject to a security interest in another jurisdiction when it was brought into this state.

☐ which is proceeds of the original collateral described above in which a security interest was perfected:

Check ☒ if covered: ☐ Proceeds of Collateral are also covered. ☐ Products of Collateral are also covered. No. of additional Sheets presented:

By: ______________________ Signature(s) of Debtor(s)

By: ______________________ Signature(s) of Secured Party(ies)

(1) Filing Officer Copy-Alphabetical **STANDARD FORM - FORM UCC-1.** (For Use In Most States)

Term Loan Agreement

THIS AGREEMENT is made this ________ day of ________________ 19 ________, by and betweer CITYBANK with a principal office at 19510 58th Ave. W., Lynnwood, Washington 98036 ("Bank") and ________________ ________________ a business having an office a: ________________ Bus. Phone # ________________ ("Borrower")

1. **LOANS, TERMS AND PURPOSE**

1.1 COMMITMENT Borrower has requested that Bank make a loan to Borrower of up to the principal sum of $________ ("Loan") and subject to the terms and conditions of this Loan Agreement, Bank agrees to lend to Borrower that amount. Such Loan shall be evidenced by a promissory note(s) in such form as shall be prescribed by Bank and will be available with the signing of this Loan Agreement and note(s), and upon fulfillment of the terms and conditions there in. This agreement shall apply to any extensions, modifications, or renewals of indebtedness hereunder.

1.2 PRINCIPAL The principal amount of the loan shall be repayable as follows: ________________.

____

1.3 INTEREST Interest on the unpaid balance of principal shall be computed on a ________ day basis at ________% or a variable rate equal to the Banks prime lending rate plus ________%. Changes in the prime rate shall be effective on the day of change. Such rate shall not be less than ________%.

1.4 OPTIONAL PREPAYMENT Borrower may at any time prepay the note(s), in whole or in part, without premium or penalty.

1.5 COLLATERAL AND DOCUMENTATION Borrower's Obligations to Bank and the collateral to be used as security for repayment thereof shall be evidenced by such notes, instruments, security agreements, and guaranties as may be required by Bank.

1.6 PURPOSE The proceeds of the loan shall be used by Borrower solely for the following purpose:

____

1.7 FEES As an inducement to Bank to make these funds available, Borrower agrees to pay an annual commitment fee of $________ which will be payable in advance. Any renewals, extensions, or modifications thereof shall be assessed on additional commitment fee not to exceed ________% of the principal loan amount outstanding.

1.8 TERM OF LOAN AGREEMENT Term of Loan agreement subject to earlier termination pursuant to the terms and conditions of this loan agreement, Banks agreement to advance funds shall terminate ________ 19 ________. At the option of the Bank, Bank agrees to renew this agreement under the following terms and conditions:

____

All other terms and conditions of this agreement remain the same.

1.9 ADDITIONAL COLLATERAL This loan is secured by the following additional collateral:

____

2. **REPRESENTATIONS AND WARRANTIES** In consideration of the loan, Borrower represents and warrants to Bank as of the date hereof and as of the date of each advance that:

2.1 LEGAL EXISTENCE Borrower is a corporation (or partnership, if applicable) duly organized and existing under the laws of the State of Washington and is duly qualified and authorized to do business in each state in which borrower does business.

2.2 VALID OBLIGATION Borrower has all necessary authority under its corporate charter or if a partnership under its partnership articles, to execute and deliver this Loan Agreement, and any notes, security agreements, instruments, and other documents to be issued hereunder by Borrower and all will be legal, valid and binding obligations of Borrower in accordance with their terms.

2.3 NO VIOLATION The making and the performance of this Loan Agreement does not violate any provision of law, or any article or bylaw of Borrower or any agreement binding on Borrower.

2.4 NO LITIGATION There is no litigation pending nor to the knowledge of Borrower threatened against Borrower that could materially and adversely affect the financial condition or continued operation of Borrower.

[page 2]

2.5 CORRECTNESS OF FINANCIAL STATEMENTS The financial statements dated ______________, previously submitted to Bank by Borrower correctly reflect Borrower's financial condition as of that date, and there have been no material adverse changes in Borrower's financial condition or operations since the date of those financial statements.

2.6 TAXES Borrower has filed all tax returns required by law to have been filed by it and has paid all taxes and governmental charges required by law to have been paid by it.

2.7 TITLE OF ASSETS Borrower has good title to its assets and they are not subject to any liens or encumbrances other than those indicated in the financial statements delivered to Bank.

2.8 NO DEFAULT Borrower is not in default of any obligation, law, governmental regulation or court decree or order materially affecting its property or business or aware of any facts of circumstances which would give rise to any such default.

2.9 INFORMATION Any information furnished and to be furnished by Borrower under this Loan Agreement are and will be true and correct in every material respect, and do not and will not omit any information necessary to provide a true and clear representation.

3. **CONDITIONS PRECEDENT** The obligation of Bank to make the loan hereunder is subject to the following conditions:

3.1 COMPLIANCE Borrower at the time of the loan shall have complied with all the covenants, representations and warranties under this Loan Agreement, and no event of default shall have occurred and be continuing at the time of the loan.

3.2 DOCUMENTATION. Borrower shall have granted and delivered to Bank in form and substance satisfactory to Bank such notes, loan security documentation and guaranties as Bank may require; and, that Borrower shall have provided Bank authenticated copies of the corporate records of Borrower and each corporate guarantor, if any, reflecting that the execution, delivery and performance of this Loan Agreement have been duly approved by the board of directors of Borrower and any corporate guarantors.

4. **AFFIRMATIVE COVENANTS OF BORROWER** Borrower covenants and agrees that so long as Borrower is indebted to Bank, Borrower will:

4.1 PUNCTUAL PAYMENT Punctually pay to Bank the interest and principal of all notes at the times and place and in the manner specified in the notes and this Loan Agreement.

4.2 ACCOUNTING RECORDS Maintain adequate books and accounts on a consistent basis in accordance with generally accepted accounting principles, and permit any representative of Bank at any reasonable time to inspect, audit and examine such books and inspect the property of Borrower.

4.3 FINANCIAL STATEMENTS Furnish within 90 days after each fiscal year a report of Borrower's financial condition and results of its operations prepared by independent certified accountants of recognized standing approved by Bank; and furnish within 45 days after each of the first three quarters of Borrower's fiscal year an unaudited financial statement prepared by Borrower, certified by Borrower's financial officer, and satisfactory to Bank, consisting of at least a balance sheet as of the close of that quarter and statement of earnings and their source and the application of funds for that quarter for the period from the beginning of that fiscal year to the close of that quarter. Bank may require Borrower to furnish audited annual financial statements prepared at Borrower's expense.

4.4 INSURANCE Maintain and keep in force insurance of the type and in amounts customarily carried in similar lines of business including adequate amounts of fire, and extended coverages, public liability, property damage, workmen's compensation, and other such insurance as Bank may reasonably require, all insurance to be carried in companies and in amounts satisfactory to Bank.

4.5 GOVERNMENTAL REGULATIONS Comply with all applicable laws and regulations of governmental agencies to the best of Borrowers ability.

4.6 MAINTENANCE OF CORPORATE EXISTANCE Preserve all corporate (or partnership, if applicable) rights, privileges and franchises, if any, and conduct the business of Borrower in an orderly manner without voluntary interruption.

4.7 LITIGATION Promptly give notice in writing to Bank of any litigation pending or threatened affecting Borrower.

4.8 TAXES AND LIABILITIES Pay and discharge all taxes, assessments, and other liabilities when due, except as contested in good faith and by appropriate proceedings.

5. **NEGATIVE COVENANTS OF BORROWER** Borrower covenants and agrees that so long as it is indebted to Bank, Borrower shall not, without prior written consent of Bank:

5.1 NO DIVERSION OF PROCEEDS Use any of the proceeds of the loan except for the purpose stated in section 1.
5.2 WORKING CAPITAL REQUIREMENT Permit working capital (excess of current assets over current liabilities) to decline below $______________ current assets and current liabilities to be determined in accordance with generally accepted accaounting principles and practices.

5.3 NET WORTH REQUIREMENTS Permit net worth to decline below $________________ net worth to be determined in accordance with generally accepted accounting principles and practices.

5.4 CAPITAL RATIO Permit Capital Ratio to exceed at any time __________ to 1. The term "Capital Ratio" means the ratio determined by dividing all of the Borrower's liabilities by Borrower's Net Worth, both to be determined in accordance with generally accepted accounting principles.

[page 3]

5.5 CAPITAL EXPENDITURE LIMITATION Make any additional investments in fixed assets or incur obligations for the lease or hire of property in any one fiscal year in excess of $________________________.

5.6 COMPENSATION Pay to any corporate officer (or partners if Borrower is partnership) any salaries, including bonuses, commissions, dividends or any other form of consideration in any fiscal year in excess of $______________, or in the aggregate not to exceed $______________.

5.7 OTHER INDEBTEDNESS Create, incur or permit to exist any liabilities resulting from borrowing, loans or advances, whether secured or unsecured, except short term borrowing from Bank and the liabilities of Borrower to Bank for money borrowed hereunder.

5.8 SECURITIES Purchase or redeem any shares of the capital stock of Borrower, declare or pay any dividends thereon other than stock dividends, or make any distribution to shareholders.

5.9 MERGER, ACQUISITION OR DISSOLUTION Purchase or otherwise acquire the assets or business of any other person or entity, nor liquidate or dissolve, merge or consolidate with any other person or entity by purchase, sale or otherwise.

5.10 GUARANTIES Guarantee or become liable in any way as surety, endorser or accommodation maker or endorser or otherwise for the debt or obligations of any other person or entity.

5.11 OWNERSHIP Make any substantial change in the management personnel of Borrower or ownership of the partnership if Borrower is a partnership.

5.12 CHANGE IN NAME OR LOCATION OF COLLATERAL Borrower agrees that if its business name is ever changed or if Borrower otherwise substantially changes its identity or corporate structure, Borrower will immediately give written notice to Bank of such change. Borrower also agrees to immediately give Bank written notice if the location of the collateral securing Borrower's indebtedness to Bank or if Borrower's books and records shall change from the location established at the execution of this Loan Agreement. Borrower further agrees that it will not remove any collateral or its books and records from the State of Washington for any reason without the prior express written consent of Bank.

6. **EVENTS OF DEFAULT** Each of the following shall constitute an Event of Default under this Loan Agreement, the occurrence of which shall, at the option of Bank, make all sums of interest and principal remaining unpaid immediately due and payable without demand, notice or presentation, all of which are expressly waived by Borrower, and shall terminate any existing loan commitment:

6.1 NONPAYMENT OF INTEREST OR PRINCIPAL Nonpayment of interest or principal according to the terms of this Loan Agreement or to the terms of any note.

6.2 BREACH OF WARRANTY The breach of any representation or warranty made by Borrower in this Loan Agreement in any material respect.

6.3 BREACH OF COVENANT Any default by Borrower under any other covenant or provision contained in this Loan Agreement or any other agreement between Borrower and Bank.

6.4 OTHER AGREEMENTS Failure to pay other indebtedness for money borrowed in excess of $___ ______________, in the aggregate, and such default shall not be cured or waived within 30 days.

6.5 BANKRUPTCY OR INSOLVENCY The insolvency of Borrower, an admission in writing of its inability to pay debts as they mature, the institution by or against Borrower of any Bankruptcy, reorganization, debt arrangement, or other proceeding under any bankruptcy or involvency law or any dissolution or liquidation proceeding.

6.6 MATERIAL ADVANCE CHANGE Any event shall occur which, in the judgment of Bank, has a materially adverse effect upon the business or the financial condition of Borrower.

7. **REMEDIES UPON DEFAULT** Upon the occurence of any event of default, Bank's obligation to make loans or extend credit hereunder shall terminate at once. In addition, Bank shall have each and all of the rights and remedies provided for by the laws of the State of Washington, this Loan Agreement, and the notes, instruments, security agreements, and guaranties provided for herein.

8. **MISCELLANEOUS**

8.1 WAIVER AND AMENDMENTS No delay on the part of Bank in the exercise of any right, power, or remedy shall operate as a waiver thereof, nor shall any single or partial exercise by Bank of any right, power or remedy preclude other or further exercise thereof or the exercise of any other right, power or remedy. No amendment, modification or waiver of, or consent with respect to, any provision of this Loan Agreement or the note shall be effective unless it shall be in writing and signed and delivered by Bank.

8.2 NOTICES All notices, requests and demands shall be given to or made upon the respective parties in writing at the following address:

If to Borrower, then to:

If to Bank, then to:..........

[page 4]

8.3 COSTS AND ATTORNEYS FEES Borrower further agrees to pay Bank all costs and expenses, including attorney's fees, incurred by Bank in collecting payment of any indebtedness and in enforcing the terms of this Loan Agreement whether or not a lawsuit is commenced. Attorney fees shall include services rendered at both the trial and appellate levels, as well as services rendered subsequent to judgment and obtaining execution thereon. The award of such fees, costs and expenses shall bear interest at the highest lawful rate until paid in full.

8.4 WASHINGTON LAW APPLICABLE This Loan Agreement and loan and the notes shall be construed in accordance with the laws of the State of Washington.

8.5 RIGHT OF SET-OFF Upon the occurrence and during the continuance of an Event of Default, Bank is hereby authorized, without notice to Borrower (any such notice being expressly waived by Borrower) to set off and apply any and all deposits of Borrower, time or demand, against any and all of the obligations of Borrower now or hereafter existing under this Loan Agreement and Note.

8.6 SURVIVAL OF WARRANTIES All agreements, representation, warranties and covenants made herein shall continue and survive the execution of this Loan Agreement and the making of any loans hereunder.

8.7 SEVERABILITY In case any provision of this Loan Agreement shall be determined to be invalid, illegal or unenforceable, such provision shall be severable from the rest of this Loan Agreement ano the validity, legality, and enforceability of the remaining provisions shall not in any way be affected or impaired thereby.

8.8 BANK ACCOUNTS As further security for repayment of amounts lent hereunder, so long as Borrower is indebted to Bank, it will maintain its principal depository accounts with Bank.

8.9 RIDERS Attached Riders, if any, are incorporated herein by reference.

IN WITNESS WHEREOF, the parties hereto have caused this Loan Agreement to be executed the day and year first hereinabove written.

____

BORROWER NAME

BY______________________________

TITLE

BY______________________________

TITLE

BY______________________________

TITLE

BY______________________________

TITLE

BY______________________________

TITLE

INDIVIDUAL FINANCIAL STATEMENT

To: ______________________________ (Lender)
Name ______________________ Date ______________, 19 ____
Address ______________________________
Social Security No. ______________ Date of Birth ______________
Occupation ______________ Employer ______________
No. of Dependents ______________ Home Phone ________ Business Phone ________

CHECK AS APPLICABLE — Applicant is applying for this loan:

☐ ALONE, without a co-signer or guaranty of a relative or other person(s) or entity.

☐ WITH A PERSON OR PERSONS who will also be contractually liable.

Names of other Person(s) ______________________________

FINANCIAL CONDITION AS OF ______________, 19 ____

ASSETS			LIABILITIES		TOTAL LIABILITY	MO. PMT. AMOUNT
Cash	Deposits with Lender		**Notes Payable to Banks**	**SCHEDULE D**		
	Other Banks			Payable to This Lender		
Stocks & Bonds	**SCHEDULE B**			Payable to Other Banks		
	Listed		**Other Notes & Accounts Payable**	**SCHEDULE D**		
	Unlisted			Contract Purchases		
Notes, Contracts & Accounts Receivable	**SCHEDULE C**			Open & Revolving Accounts		
				Other		
			Taxes Payable	Income Taxes		
				R/E Taxes		
Life Ins.	Cash Value		**Real Estate, Notes & Contracts Payable**	**SCHEDULE D**		
Real Estate	**SCHEDULE A**			Residences(s)		
	Residence(s)			Unimproved Land		
	Unimproved Land			Income Property		
	Income Property			Other		
	Other		**Other Liabilities**	**SCHEDULE D**		
Other Personal Property	**SCHEDULE E**			Life Ins. Loans		
	Autos & Trucks					
	Furniture & Fixtures					
Other Assets	**SCHEDULE E**					
				TOTAL LIABILITIES		
				NET WORTH		
	TOTAL ASSETS			**TOTAL**		

RE-CAP OF INCOME AND EXPENSES

ANNUAL INCOME FOR YEAR 19 ____		ANNUAL EXPENSES FOR YEAR 19 ____		CONTINGENT LIABILITIES	
Salary or Wages		Property Tax & Assessments		As Endorser on Notes/Contracts	
Dividends or Interest		Fed. & State Income Tax		As Guarantor on Notes/Contracts	
Rentals (Gross Income)		Real Estate Loan Payments		For Taxes	
Business (Net Income)		Payments on Contracts/Notes		Other (Describe)	
Other Income (Describe) *		Estimated Living Expenses			
		Other:			
TOTAL INCOME	$	TOTAL EXPENSES	$	TOTAL	$

*Alimony, child support or maintenance payment income need not be revealed if you do not wish to have it considered as a basis for repaying this obligation.

LIFE INSURANCE

FACE AMOUNT	BENEFICIARY	COMPANY

APPLICANT(S)' SIGNATURE(S)

I/we affirm that the information contained in this application is true, complete and correct and that Lender is relying on this information if it makes the requested loan. Lender is authorized to make any investigation of my/our credit and/or employment status either directly or through any agency employed by Lender. Lender may disclose to any other interested parties Lender's experience with my/our loan account. Lender may keep this application even it it decides not to make the loan to me/us.

Applicant(s)' Signature(s):

______________________ ______________________

______________________, 19 ____ ______________________, 19 ____

SPOUSAL CONSENT (If you are relying on income from your spouse or former spouse who is not an applicant above, please have your spouse or former spouse complete this section so that we may verify their credit.)
I authorize Lender to make any investigation of my credit either directly or through any agency employed by Lender for that purpose in connection with this credit application by my spouse or former spouse.

Date ____________ Signature ______________________ Social Security Number ______________

(SHORT FORM) (TUMBLE)

[reverse side]

With each schedule list below indicate co-ownership, if any, and the extent of it.

SCHEDULE A LIST OF REAL ESTATE AND IMPROVEMENTS (Show Mortgage Information in Schedule D)

Type and Location of Property	Date Acquired	Title in Name of	Holder of Lien	% You Own	Annual Taxes	Monthly Rent	Original Cost	Present Market Value

SCHEDULE B STOCKS AND BONDS

Number of Shares	Description — Rate — Maturity If Pledged, to Whom	How Registered	Market Value	Book Value If No Market

SCHEDULE C NOTES, CONTRACTS AND ACCOUNTS RECEIVABLE

Due from (Name)	Date of Obligation	Balance		Payment Terms	Due Date	Description of Collateral If Any
		Original	Present			

SCHEDULE D NOTES, CONTRACTS AND ACCOUNTS PAYABLE (Include Mortgages on Property Listed in Schedule A)

Due to (Name)	Date Incurred	Balance		Payment Terms	Due Date	Description of Collateral If Any
		Original	Present			

SCHEDULE E DETAILS OF OTHER IMPORTANT ASSETS

Items	Estimated Current Value	Items	Estimated Current Value	Items	Estimated Current Value

APPENDIX C

Sources of Financial Ratios

Financial ratios come from two main sources: organizations that compile financial information on a number of industries and trade associations and other publishers that primarily provide financial information on a specific industry. In the first category, there are three widely known publications: *Annual Statement Studies, Industry Norms and Key Business Ratios,* and *Almanac of Business and Industrial Financial Ratios.* Most public libraries have one or more of these publications.

Let's look at both of these sources.

Financial Data Compilers on Many Industries

Annual Statement Studies

Annual Statement Studies is published by Robert Morris and Associates (RMA), the national association of bank loan and credit officers. Each year, the 1,200 member banks of RMA supply financial statements on their customers. (The names of the companies are removed for confidentiality.) These thousands of statements are classified into one of 350 industry categories.

Industry Norms and Key Business Ratios

Dun & Bradstreet Credit Services publishes *Industry Norms and Key Business Ratios.* This publication lists financial data on over 800 businesses in five industries.

The calculations are based on the Dun's Financial Profiles data base, which contains the financial statements on over 1 million privately and publicly held companies.

Almanac of Business and Industrial Financial Ratios

The *Almanac* is published by Prentice Hall. Its focus is slightly different from either *Annual Statement Studies* or *Industry Norms and Key Business Ratios.* The reason is the *Almanac* obtains its financial information from the Internal Revenue Service (IRS).

Information from IRS returns is provided to the *Almanac,* which classifies the information into over 180 different industry categories. Within each category, the financial statements are separated by asset size. Within each of these sections, roughly 20 financial ratios are calculated.

Trade Associations and Other Publishers of Financial Data

There are thousands of different trade associations in this country. Many gather financial data on their industry and, once compiled, make this information available to their members and other interested parties.

To find the association for your type of business, look in *Encyclopedia of Associations,* available at most libraries. It contains the names and addresses of over 25,000 trade associations.

Well-known organizations that promote the availability of their financial information include the following:

Accounting and Bookkeeping

Income and Fees of Accountants in Public Practice. National Society of Public Accountants, 1010 North Fairfax Street, Alexandria, Virginia 22314.

Advertising

Advertising Age. Crain Communications, Inc., 740 North Rush Street, Chicago, Illinois 60611.

Aerospace

Aerospace Facts and Figures. Compiled by Aerospace Industries Association of America, Inc., 1725 DeSales Street, N.W., Washington, D.C. 20036.

Air-Conditioning and Refrigeration Equipment

Report of Operating Costs: Plumbing, Heating, Cooling, Piping Wholesalers. American Supply Association, 20 North Wacker Drive, Suite 2260, Chicago, Illinois 60606.

Airlines

Air Transport. Air Transport Association of America, 1709 New York Avenue, N.W., Washington, D.C. 20006.

Apparel

Annual Business Survey. Menswear Retailers of America, 2011 I Street, N.W., Suite 600, Washington, D.C. 20006.
Special Statistical Report on Profit, Sales and Production Trends of the Men's and Boy's Clothing Industry. Clothing Manufacturers Association of the U.S.A., 1290 Avenue of the Americas, Suite 1351, New York, New York 10104.

Automobile Dealers

NADA DATA: Economic Impact of America's New Car and Truck Dealers. National Automobile Dealers Association, 8400 Westpark Drive, McLean, Virginia 22102.

Aviation Maintenance

AMFI Industry Report. Aviation Maintenance Foundations, P.O. Box 2826, Redmond, Washington 98073.

Collection Agencies

Cost of Operations Survey. American Collectors Association, Inc., 4040 West 70th Street, Minneapolis, Minnesota 55435.

Computer Software

Operating Ratios Survey for the Computer Software and Services Industry. ADAPSO (Computer Software and Services Industry Association), Suite 300, 1300 North 17th Street, Arlington, Virginia 22209.

Country Clubs

Clubs in Town and Country. Pannell Kerr Forster, 262 North Belt East, Suite 300, Houston, Texas 77060.

Data Processing Services

Wage and Salary Study. ADAPSO (Computer Software and Services Industry Association), Suite 300, 1300 North 17th Street, Arlington, Virginia 22209.

Department Stores

Financial and Operating Results of Department and Specialty Stores. National Retail Merchants Association, 100 West 31st Street, New York, New York 10001.

Operating Results of Self-Service Discount Department Stores. Cornell University, 205 Warren Hall, Ithaca, New York 14853.

Distributors (Industrial)

Distributor Productivity Report. National Industrial Distributors Association, 1900 Arch Street, Philadelphia, Pennsylvania 19103.

Drugstores

The Lilly Digest. Eli Lilly and Company, 307 East McCarty Street, Indianapolis, Indiana 46285.

NACDS-Lilly Digest: A Survey of Chain Pharmacy Operations. Eli Lilly and Company, 307 East McCarty Street, Indianapolis, Indiana 46285.

NWDA Operating Survey. National Wholesale Druggists' Association, P.O. Box 238, Alexandria, Virginia 22313.

Supermarket Pharmacies. Food Marketing Institute, 1750 K Street, N.W., Washington, D.C. 20006.

Electrical Contractors

Financial Performance Report. National Electrical Contractors Association, 7315 Wisconsin Avenue, Bethesda, Maryland 20814.

Electrical Manufacturers

Annual Financial and Operating Ratios for Electrical Manufacturing Industry. National Electrical Manufacturers Association, 2101 L Street, N.W., Suite 300, Washington, D.C. 20037.

Farm and Power Equipment

Cost of Doing Business—Farm and Power Equipment Dealers. National Farm & Power Equipment Dealers Association, 10877 Watson Road, St. Louis, Missouri 63127.

Florists

FTD Operating Survey. Florists' Transworld Delivery Association, 29200 Northwestern Highway, Southfield, Michigan 48037.

Furniture Retailers

NHFA Operating Experiences. National Home Furnishing Association, 405 Merchandise Mart, Chicago, Illinois 60654.

Gambling

Study of Financial Results and Reporting Trends in the Gaming Industry. Laventhol & Horwath, 1845 Walnut Street, Philadelphia, Pennsylvania 19103.

Gas Utility Companies

Gas Facts. American Gas Association, 1515 Wilson Boulevard, Arlington, Virginia 22209.

Groceries

Annual Financial Review. Food Marketing Institute, 1750 K Street, N.W., Washington, D.C. 20006.

Facts about Store Development. Food Marketing Institute, 1750 K Street, N.W., Washington, D.C. 20006.

Food Marketing Industry Speaks. Food Marketing Institute, 1750 K Street, N.W., Washington, D.C. 20006.

Operations Review. Food Marketing Institute, 1750 K Street, N.W., Washington, D.C. 20006.

Hardware Retailers

The Bottom Line. National Retail Hardware Association, 770 North High School Road, Indianapolis, Indiana 46224.

Management Report. National Retail Hardware Association, 770 North High School Road, Indianapolis, Indiana 46224.

Hospitals

Hospital Industry Financial Report. Healthcare Financial Management Association, 1900 Spring Road, Suite 500, Oak Brook, Illinois 60521.

Lilly Hospital Pharmacy Survey. Eli Lilly and Company, 307 East McCarty Street, Indianapolis, Indiana 46285.

Hotels and Motels

California Lodging Industry. Laventhol & Horwath, 1845 Walnut Street, Philadelphia, Pennsylvania 19103.

Canada Trend of Business in Hotels. Laventhol & Horwath, 1845 Walnut Street, Philadelphia, Pennsylvania 19103.

National Trend of Business in the Lodging Industry. Laventhol & Horwath, 1845 Walnut Street, Philadelphia, Pennsylvania 19103.

Trends in the Hotel Industry. Pannell Kerr Forster, 262 North Belt East, Suite 300, Houston, Texas 77060.

U.S. Economy Lodging Industry. Laventhol & Horwath, 1845 Walnut Street, Philadelphia, Pennsylvania 19103.

Meat and Meat Products

Annual Financial Operating Survey of the Meat Industry. American Meat Institute, P.O. Box 3556, Washington, D.C. 20007.

Medical Group Practices

MGMA Annual Cost and Production Survey Report. Medical Group Management Association, 1355 South Colorado Boulevard, Suite 900, Denver, Colorado 80222.

Metal Treating

Metal Treating Institute Operational Cost Survey. Metal Treating Institute, 300 North 2d Street, Suite 11, Jacksonville Beach, Florida 32250.

Mortgage Banking

Mortgage Banking: Financial Statements and Operating Ratios. Mortgage Bankers Association of America, 1125 15th Street, N.W., Washington, D.C. 20005.

Motor Carriers

Motor Carrier Annual Reports. American Trucking Associations, Inc., 2200 Mill Road, Alexandria, Virginia 22314.

Nursing Homes

Lifecare Industry. Laventhol & Horwath, 1845 Walnut Street, Philadelphia, Pennsylvania 19103.

Office Products

NOPA Dealer Operating Results. National Office Products Association, 301 North Fairfax Street, Alexandria, Virginia 22314.

Packaging

The Annual Key Ratio Survey of the Folding Carton and Rigid Box Industry. National Paperbox and Packaging Association, 231 Kings Highway East, Haddonfield, New Jersey 08033.

Paper

The Paper Distribution Industry: A Market Research Data Source. National Paper Trade Association, Inc., 111 Great Neck Road, Great Neck, New York 11021.

Paper Merchant Performance. National Paper Trade Association, Inc., 111 Great Neck Road, Great Neck, New York 11021.

Statistics of Paper and Paperboard. American Paper Institute, 269 Madison Avenue, New York, New York 10016.

Petroleum Marketing

Petroleum Marketing Databook. Petroleum Marketing Education Foundation, 101 North Alfred Street, Suite 200, Alexandria, Virginia 22314.

Plumbing and Heating Equipment

Report of Operating Costs: Plumbing, Heating, Cooling, Piping Wholesalers. American Supply Association, 20 North Wacker Drive, Suite 2260, Chicago, Illinois 60606.

The Wholesaler, Profit & Market Survey. 135 Addison Avenue, Elmhurst, Illinois 60126.

Power, Fluid (Wholesalers)

Annual Distributor Productivity Report. Fluid Power Distributors Association, 1900 Arch Street, Philadelphia, Pennsylvania 19103.

Printing and Publishing

NAQP Wage & Benefits Survey. National Association of Quick Printers, 111 East Wacker Drive, Chicago, Illinois 60601.

Operating Ratio Study. National Association of Quick Printers, 111 East Wacker Drive, Chicago, Illinois 60601.

Operating Ratios for the Typographic Industry. Typographers International Association, 2262 Hall Place, N.W., Washington, D.C. 20007.

Printing Industries of America, Inc., Annual Financial Ratio Studies. Printing Industries of America, Inc., Financial Services Department, 1730 North Lynn Street, Arlington, Virginia 22209.

Racquet Sports

Profiles of Success: State of the Industry Report. International Racquet Sports Association, 132 Brookline Avenue, Boston, Massachusetts 02215.

Radio and Television Stations

Radio Financial Report. National Association of Broadcasters, 1771 N Street, N.W., Washington, D.C. 20036.

Television Financial Report. National Association of Broadcasters, 1771 N Street, N.W., Washington, D.C. 20036.

Railroads

Railroad Revenues, Expenses, and Income. Association of American Railroads, 50 F Street, N.W., Room 5401, Washington, D.C. 20001.

Real Estate

BOMA Experience Exchange Report. Building Owners and Managers Association International, 1250 I Street, N.W., Washington, D.C. 20005.
Dollars and Cents of Shopping Centers. Urban Land Institute, 1090 Vermont Avenue, N.W., Washington, D.C. 20005.

Refrigeration Wholesalers

Overhead Expense Figures for the Calendar or Fiscal Year. National Commercial Refrigeration Sales Association, 1900 Arch Street, Philadelphia, Pennsylvania 19103.

Restaurants

California Restaurant Operations. Laventhol & Horwath, 1845 Walnut Street, Philadelphia, Pennsylvania 19103.
Operating Results of Food Chains. Cornell University, 205 Warren Hall, Ithaca, New York 14853.
Restaurant Industry Operations Report. National Restaurant Association, 311 First Street, N.W., Washington, D.C. 20001.
Survey of Wage Rates for Hourly Employees. National Restaurant Association, 311 First Street, N.W., Washington, D.C. 20001.

Savings Institutions

Savings Institutions Sourcebook. United States League of Savings Institutions, 111 East Wacker Drive, Chicago, Illinois 60691.

Shoe Retailers

Shoe Store Operational Study. National Shoe Retailers Association, 1414 Avenue of the Americas, New York, New York 10019.

Sporting Goods

Cost of Doing Business Survey. National Sporting Goods Association, 1699 Wall Street, Mt. Prospect, Illinois 60056.

Telephone and Telegraph Communication

Telephone Statistics. Vol. 1. United States Telephone Association, 900 19th Street, N.W., Suite 800, Washington, D.C. 20006.

Tennis Clubs

Industry Data Survey. International Racquet Sports Association, 132 Brookline Avenue, Boston, Massachusetts 02215.

Truck Equipment Retailers

Distributors Operating Results Survey Report. National Truck Equipment Association, 25900 Greenfield Road, Suite 410, Oak Park, Michigan 48237.

Trucking

Financial and Operating Statistics. American Trucking Associations, Inc., 2200 Mill Road, Alexandria, Virginia 22314.

Vending Machine Operators

Cost and Profit Ratios for Vending Operators. National Automatic Merchandising Association, 20 North Wacker Drive, Suite 3500, Chicago, Illinois 60606.

Vending and Food Service Management. National Automatic Merchandising Association, 20 North Wacker Drive, Suite 3500, Chicago, Illinois 60606.

Video Software

VSDA Annual Survey. Video Software Dealers Association, 1008-F Astoria Boulevard, Cherry Hill, New Jersey 08003.

Glossary

account payable A current liability representing the amount owed to a creditor for merchandise or services purchased on an open account. (Excessive accounts payable may mean that a company could experience difficulties paying creditors in the future.)

account receivable A current asset representing the amount owed by a debtor for merchandise or services purchased on an open account.

accrual basis The accounting practice whereby income and expenses are recorded when they occur, although the cash may not be received or paid until later.

accrued income Income earned during a fiscal period but not paid by the end of the period.

administrative expenses Expenses charged to the managerial aspect of running a business.

aging of accounts receivable A grouping of customer accounts according to due dates.

allowance for depreciation An accumulated expense that writes off the cost of a fixed asset over its estimated useful life. The allowance does not necessarily reflect the decline in the value of the asset.

amortization The gradual reduction of a debt by the making of equal periodic payments so the debt will be paid off by maturity. For example, a debt amortized over 20 years would be paid off at the end of 20 years.

annual percentage rate (APR) The finance charge on a loan over a one-year period expressed as a percentage. (Depending on the amount borrowed, a slightly lower APR can save the borrower a considerable amount of money.)

appraisal fee The charge for estimating the value of an asset.

appreciation The increase in the value of an asset above its cost due to inflation or economic conditions.

APR *See* annual percentage rate.

asset Anything owned by an individual or a business that has commercial or exchange value, such as inventory, accounts receivable, and equipment.

average daily balance The average amount of money that a customer keeps in an account. It is determined by adding the daily balances of the account over a given period of time and then dividing the total by the days covered.

average inventory The approximate amount of merchandise on hand during a given period. (There are several ways to value inventory.)

bad debts The amount of accounts receivable that are uncollectible. (The inability to collect receivables is a common problem of companies with financial problems.)

balance sheet An itemized statement for an individual or business that lists the assets, liabilities, and difference between the two (called the *net worth*).

balloon payment Any lump-sum payment that is more than the normally scheduled payment amount. (Sometimes term loans call for a balloon payment at the end of one year.)

bank credit card A card issued by a bank that allows the customer to buy goods and services and pay the bank later. MasterCard and Visa are the two most widely accepted bank credit cards.

bank examiner A reviewer of loans made by lending personnel. The bank examiner verifies that the loans are made in accordance with existing guidelines, policies, and procedures.

break-even point The sales activity needed at which no profit or loss is generated. (For start-up companies, some banks like to see a break-even analysis included in the written loan proposal.)

budget An itemized listing of revenues and expenses to be generated over a specified time.

capital budget The amount available for the purchase of fixed assets during a given period of time.

capital stock The ownership shares of a corporation authorized by its articles of incorporation.

cash basis The practice of recording revenues and expenses only when cash is actually received or paid.

cash control A system of verifying the accuracy of all cash receipts and disbursements.

cash discount A deduction from the selling price permitted by the seller to encourage earlier payment on an invoice. (When possible, it is usually wise to take cash discounts. Over time, the amount of savings can be considerable.)

cash flow The difference between cash receipts and disbursements over a given period of time. Some people use this term to refer to the net profits plus noncash expenses (such as depreciation) earned by a company. (Research shows that cash flow difficulties cause more bankruptcies than lack of profits.)

charge-off A bookkeeping loss to the lender because the amount owed was not collected from the debtor. (The average charge-off rate in the commercial banking industry is about 1.5 percent of outstanding loans.)

collateral An asset pledged to a creditor to ensure repayment of a debt. Should repayment not be made in a timely manner, the lender may repose and sell the collateral to retire the obligation. (As a rule of thumb, when using an item as collateral, bankers prefer to lend 80 percent or less of its market value.)

commercial bank A federal or state-chartered corporation that provides a range of banking services.

commercial loan A loan primarily made to a business to assist in its financing needs. (There are four basic types of commercial business loans: business cycle, working capital, term, and interim loan.)

consolidation loan A loan that combines or consolidates several debts into a single loan.

corporation A type of business organization chartered by a state and given many of the legal rights of a separate entity.

cosigner A person other than the borrower who signs a promissory note and is equally responsible for paying back the bank. A cosigner provides additional protection to the creditor that the debt will be repaid.

credit An agreement to receive money, goods, or services now while paying for them in the future. (When a loan is granted, the bank is the creditor and the borrower the debtor.)

credit analysis The process of evaluating an applicant's borrowing request.

credit bureau A reporting agency that collects credit information on an ongoing basis from firms that grant credit and from public records. This information is available to the bureau's membership for a fee.

credit department A department within a bank where credit information is obtained, assembled, and retained for reference purposes.

credit file A folder where all credit information on a borrowing customer is assembled.

credit history A record of a borrower's debts and payment habits. (A record of good credit is usually a prerequisite for borrowing money from a bank.)

credit life insurance Insurance that will pay the unpaid balance of a customer's debts in case of death. (Before buying this insurance, it is a good idea to get a competitive bid from an insurance agent.)

credit report A report compiled by a credit bureau that lists information provided by credit-granting organizations.

creditworthiness The ability and willingness of a person to repay his or her debts.

current assets Items owned by an individual or business that are normally converted into cash within a year. Cash, accounts receivable, and inventory are examples.

current liabilitities Items owed by an individual or business that are normally expected to be paid within a year. Accounts payable, notes payable, and the current portion of long-term debt are examples.

current ratio A ratio that measures solvency. It can be determined by dividing current assets by current liabilities. (All bankers look at a company's current ratio when analyzing a financial statement.) *See also* working capital ratio.

debtor A person or firm owing money, goods, or services to another.

debt-to-worth ratio A ratio that measures the amount of leverage used by the owners or stockholders of a company. It is defined as total liabilities divided by net worth. (The higher is the debt-to-worth ratio, the higher is the risk for both creditors and the owner.)

default Failure to meet any of the terms outlined in a credit agreement.

delinquent loan A loan for which payment is past due and no arrangements have been made with the bank. (If your loan is delinquent, it is always best to contact your banker before he contacts you.)

depreciation An adjustment to the bookkeeping value of an asset that theoretically reflects its declining value.

dividend That portion of a corporation's earnings paid to stockholders. Rapidly growing companies usually do not pay dividends because the company's profits are used to finance future growth.

equity *See* net worth.

Federal Deposit Insurance Corporation A government corporation that insures the deposits of selected banks. The deposits in these institutions are entitled to the benefits of insurance under the Federal Reserve Act.

finance charges The cost of a loan in actual dollars and cents, as required by the federal Truth-in-Lending Act of 1968.

fixed assets Assets that normally will not be converted into cash during the coming year. Plant and equipment are examples.

fixed costs Costs that remain relatively constant in the operation of a business and do not vary with fluctuations in sales. Rent, insurance, and utilities are examples.

gross margin ratio A ratio that shows the percentage of sales dollars left after deducting the cost of goods sold. It can be found by dividing the gross profit by total sales.

gross profit on sales The amount by which the net sales exceed the cost of goods sold.

guarantor A person legally obligated to pay back a loan if the borrower defaults. (Bankers commonly ask major stockholders to guarantee loans made to corporations.)

income statement The profit and loss statement for a business over a certain period of time.

installment loan A loan for which the borrower makes regular payments (usually monthly) of equal amounts to a creditor.

insurance premium An amount paid to an insurance company for a specific type and amount of insurance.

intangible assets Items of a nonphysical nature that are of value to a business. Examples are goodwill, patents, and trademarks.

leverage Borrowing money from others to acquire assets. (As the leverage of a firm increases, so does the risk to both creditors and owner.)

liabilities Debts of a person or a business. Accounts payable, notes payable, and mortgages are examples.

lien A creditor's legal right to confiscate and sell assigned collateral to pay off the debtor's obligation.

line of credit An agreement between a bank and a customer whereby the bank agrees to lend the customer an amount of money with a specific upper limit (such as $100,000). A line of credit may be secured or unsecured. It is usually established when the borrower has frequent borrowing need.

liquidating value The anticipated amount of money that would be received from the sale of an asset in the case of a forced liquidation. Many times the liquidation value is less than 50 percent of the value listed on the balance sheet.

liquidity A term used to describe the solvency of a person or business. The ease with which assets can be converted into cash is an indication of liquidity.

loan officer An officer of the bank with the responsibility of approving and declining loan applications.

long-term debt An obligation not due within the next year.

maturity The date upon which a loan or credit line is due in full. Loans often are written with a maturity of 90 days, 120 days, or a year.

mortgage A written obligation to pay a debt with property pledged as collateral.

net income The excess of revenues over expenses for a fiscal period.

net profit margin ratio A ratio that reflects the percentage of sales dollars left after deducting all expenses except income taxes. It can be determined by dividing total sales into the net profit before taxes.

net sales The amount of sales during a period after making adjustments for returns and sales discounts.

net worth The difference between total assets and total liabilities. Sometimes referred to as *equity* or *owner's equity.*

note *See* promissory note.

notes payable A written promise to pay a certain amount by a given date.

notes receivable A written promise by another party to pay a certain amount by a given date.

obligation A debt.

outstanding balance The remaining amount to pay on a loan as of a specific date. Sometimes referred to as *principal balance owing.*

overdraft A negative balance in the checking account that occurs when more money is taken out than is in the account. (Bankers don't like overdrafts; it's an unwritten rule of banking.)

partnership A legal arrangement of two or more people for the purpose of operating a business. Legally, the owners are personally liable for the risks of the business venture.

personal financial statement An individual's listing of personal assets, liabilities, and net worth as of a given date. (Most bankers like to receive an updated personal financial statement on borrowing customers annually.)

points A fee charged by a lending institution to adjust the cost of the loan to market conditions. One point is equal to 1 percent of the principal dollar amount. Points can be negotiated.

prime rate The rate of interest the bank charges its most creditworthy customers.

principal The amount of a loan, excluding any finance charges. Sometimes the principal amount owing is referred to as the *outstanding balance.*

principal balance owing *See* outstanding balance.

pro forma A projection or estimate of future business. (Bankers often request a pro forma income statement, cash budget, and pro forma balance sheet.)

promissory note A written document that is legal evidence of a debt. The debtor promises to pay a specific amount of money plus finance charges by a certain date or on demand. Frequently referred to as a *note.*

quick ratio A ratio that measures liquidity. It is defined as cash plus accounts receivable divided by current liabilities.

return on assets (ROA) A ratio that measures how efficiently profits are being generated for the assets employed in the business. Dividing the net profit before taxes by the total assets yields the ROA ratio.

return on investment (ROI) A ratio that is a reflection of the owner's return on capital invested in the company. It can be found by dividing the net worth into the net profit before taxes.

ROA *See* return on assets.

ROI *See* return on investment.

secured loan A loan with an asset pledged as colateral. (Almost all term loans are made on a secured basis.)

signature loan A loan to an individual granted on an unsecured basis.

sole proprietorship A business organization in which one individual owns the business. Legally, the owner's personal assets are exposed to the risks of the business.

term loan A loan with a repayment period extending beyond one year. (Almost all term loans require that the borrower pledge collateral.)

unsecured loan A loan made to a person or company that does not require collateral.

usury The charging of an excessive or illegal rate of interest. (Usury rates are determined by state statue.)

working capital The difference between current assets and current liabilities. (A negative working capital position probably indicates a company is having severe problems paying its obligations.)

working capital ratio Current assets divided by current liabilities. Frequently called the *current ratio.*

Bibliography

Bel Air, Roger. *Make a Fortune Buying Discounted Mortgages.* Garden City, N.Y.: Doubleday, 1987.

Dible, Donald M. *Up Your Own Organization.* Reston, Va.: Reston Publishing Press, 1981.

Gumpert, David E., and Jeffrey A. Timmons. *The Insider's Guide to Small Business Resources.* Garden City, N.Y.: Doubleday, 1982.

Hayes, Rick Stephen. *Business Loans: A Guide to Money Sources and How to Approach Them Successfully.* New York: Van Nostrand Reinhold Co., 1980.

Hayes, Rick S., and John Howell. *How to Finance Your Small Business with Government Money.* New York: Wiley, 1983.

J. K. Lasser Tax Institute. *How to Run a Small Business.* New York: McGraw-Hill, 1984.

Myer, John N. *Financial Statement Analysis.* Englewood Cliffs, N.J.: Prentice Hall, 1969.

Osgood, William R. *How to Plan and Finance Your Business.* New York: Van Nostrand Reinhold Co., 1980.

Pratt, Stanley E. *Guide to Venture Capital Sources.* Wellesley Hills, Mass.: Capital Publishing Corporation, 1983.

Putt, William D. *How to Start Your Own Business.* Cambridge: MIT Press, 1984.

Simmons, James G. *Creative Business Financing.* Englewood Cliffs, N.J.: Prentice-Hall, 1983.

Spurga, Ronald C. *Balance Sheet Basics: Financial Management for Nonfinancial Managers.* New York: Franklin Watts, 1986.

Steinhoff, Dan. *Small Business Management Fundamentals.* New York: McGraw-Hill, 1984.

White, Jerry F., and John A. Welsh. *The Entrepreneur's Master Planning Guide.* Englewood Cliffs, N.J.: Prentice Hall, 1983.

Index